Enjoy Your Trip!
—English you need abroad—

Masumi Takeuchi　Nobumi Nakai　Chizu Sugawara

editorial support
Joseph Tabolt

NAN'UN-DO

Enjoy Your Trip!
―English you need abroad―

Copyright© 2015

by
Masumi Takeuchi Nobumi Nakai Chizu Sugawara

editorial support
Joseph Tabolt

All Rights Reserved
No part of this book may be reproduced in any form without written permission from the authors and Nan'un-do Co., Ltd.

このテキストの音声を無料で視聴（ストリーミング）・ダウンロードできます。自習用音声としてご活用ください。
以下のサイトにアクセスしてテキスト番号で検索してください。

https://nanun-do.com　　テキスト番号 [511675]

※ 無線 LAN（WiFi）に接続してのご利用を推奨いたします。

※ 音声ダウンロードは Zip ファイルでの提供になります。
　お使いの機器によっては別途ソフトウェア（アプリケーション）の導入が必要となります。

※ Enjoy Your Trip! 音声ダウンロードページは以下の
　QR コードからもご利用になれます。

はじめに

　この『Enjoy Your Trip! － English you need abroad －（旅英語の心得）』は、近い将来、英語を使って海外旅行をしてみたいと考えている日本人学習者のために書かれた英語教材です。旅は楽しいだけでなく、異なる文化に出遭い、その多様性を学習するすばらしい機会です。同時に、日常生活とは異なる種々の問題に直面する場合も出てくるでしょう。

　本教材の主たる目的は、「旅英語」すなわち、旅先での英語コミュニケーション能力の向上にあります。本書を効果的に用いて学習することによって、将来さまざまな場面で困難な状況に置かれたときに、言語の違いに阻まれて言いたいことも言えずに我慢するのではなく、ある程度のレベルのコミュニケーションを自力で行うための土台づくりができると考えています。

　本書は、旅の舞台を米国ニューヨークに設定し、旅の過程で遭遇しそうな場面をユニットごとに順番に再現しています。海外旅行の疑似体験を楽しみながら学習を進めてください。

　本書では、旅英語の三技能「聞く」「話す」「読む」を中心に学習します。各ユニットは、「Vocabulary」「Comprehension Check」「Listening」「Pronunciation」「Useful Expressions」「Reading」「Numbers」「異文化コミュニケーション／Travel Tips（日本語コラム）」「Survival Activity」、それに加え「Numbers」の復習として用意した巻末の「Pair Work with Numbers」の 10 項目で統一的に構成されています。

　本書は、三人の現役の大学英語教員が共同執筆しました。そのうち二人は異文化コミュニケーションが専門で、一人は意味論・語用論が専門です。教育現場での経験に加え、それぞれの専門知識が随所に生かされています。また、編集段階では、ニューヨーク生まれでニューヨーク育ちのアメリカ人協力者に、母語話者としてだけでなく、語用論的視点からも英語表現を検討してもらいました。

　本書最大の強みは、何といっても、著者のひとりに旅行会社での実務経験があり、渡航歴 400 回以上という豊富な旅の経験をもとに執筆されたところです。

　本書を手にとってくれた皆さんが、旅英語の学習を通じて、将来的に、旅先であってもなくても、英語を用いて積極的に意思表示や問題解決をしてみようと考えてくださるようになれば、著者一同、それに勝る喜びはありません。

Enjoy Your Trip!
著者一同
2014 年 7 月吉日

Contents

Unit 1	At the airport	7
Unit 2	On the plane	13
Unit 3	Arrival	19
Unit 4	Checking in at the hotel	25
Unit 5	Getting information and sightseeing	31
Unit 6	Ordering fast food	37
Unit 7	Going to the theater	43
Unit 8	At the restaurant	49
Unit 9	Shopping	55
Unit 10	Lost and found	61
Unit 11	Using public transportation	67
Unit 12	Renting a bike	73
Unit 13	Finding your way around	79
Unit 14	Medical care	85
Unit 15	Leaving for home	91

Additional Activities (Pair Work with Numbers)	97
Script for Comprehension Check	107

Unit 1　At the airport

🌐 Vocabulary

次の語句の意味を下から選びなさい。

1. boarding pass　(　　　)　　2. approximately　(　　　)
3. confirmation　(　　　)　　4. fee　(　　　)
5. frequent　(　　　)　　6. clerk　(　　　)
7. gadget　(　　　)　　8. liquid　(　　　)
9. departure　(　　　)　　10. row　(　　　)
11. item　(　　　)　　12. issue　(　　　)
13. fuel　(　　　)　　14. require　(　　　)
15. allowance　(　　　)

確認	小さな機械装置	おおよそ	液体	搭乗券
料金	係員、店員	項目、品目	出発	燃料
頻繁な	割当量、許可量	列	…を必要とする	…を発行する

Comprehension Check

音声を聞き、正しい答えを選びなさい。

Scene 1 <At the check-in counter>

(1) She is going to check in (two suitcases / one suitcase).

(2) She is going to (pay an extra fee / carry some items on the plane).

Scene 2 <At the security checkpoint>

(1) She is required to show her (ticket / boarding pass) to the officer.

(2) She has to take off (her coat / her shoes).

Scene 3 <At the information counter>

(1) The boarding gate has been changed from (D56 to E80 / E80 to D56).

(2) She must take (a shuttle train / a shuttle bus) to the new gate.

Listening

音声を聞き、(　　　) を埋めなさい。

Good afternoon passengers. This is the pre-boarding announcement for AB Airline flight number 123 to New York, (① 　　　　) Airport. We are now inviting those passengers with small children and any passengers requiring (② 　　　　) assistance, and Gold Sky (③ 　　　　) Flier members and first class and business class passengers, to begin boarding at this time. Please have your boarding pass and passport ready. Regular boarding for economy (④ 　　　　) will begin in approximately (⑤ 　　　　) minutes' time by row and start with the row numbers near the (⑥ 　　　　) of the plane. Thank you.

Unit 1 At the airport

◯ Pronunciation 4

次の国名・都市名を英語で書き、音声を聞いて発音しなさい。

英国　　　　　(　　　　　　)　　アメリカ合衆国　(　　　　　　)
カナダ　　　　(　　　　　　)　　オーストラリア　(　　　　　　)
ロサンジェルス　(　　　　　　)　　トロント　　　　(　　　　　　)
シドニー　　　(　　　　　　)　　メルボルン　　　(　　　　　　)

◯ Useful Expressions 5

ペアで練習しなさい。

1. (A) Can I check in now?

   (B) Sorry, could you wait another five minutes?

2. (A) Can I see your passport, please?

   (B) Yes, here you are.

3. (A) Could you remove your coat, please?

   (B) Oh yes, certainly.

4. (A) Could you open your suitcase?

   (B) Sure, just a moment please.

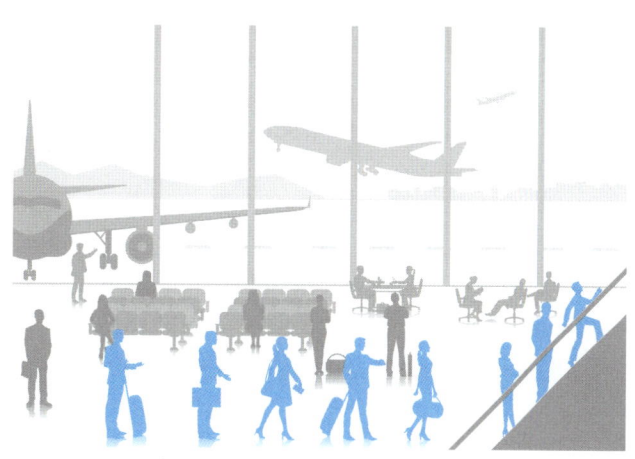

 # Reading

次の表を読み、Q1〜Q3に答えなさい。

AB Airlines E-ticket and Itinerary/Receipt

This is your E-ticket.   Your confirmation number: CKL343
Thank you for choosing AB Airlines' Electronic Ticket.

Flight	Depart	Arrive	Duration	Class	Seat
AB 123	06:50 Tokyo (HND) Sun. MAR. 01	06:30 New York (JFK) Sun. MAR. 01	12H 20MIN	Coach	35C
AB 234	06:50 New York (JFK) Sun. MAR. 08	09:55 Los Angeles (LAX) Sun. MAR.08	5H 55MIN	Coach	21B
AB 122	12:00 Los Angeles (LAX) Sun. MAR, 08	15:50+1day Tokyo (NRT) Mon. MAR. 09	11H 50MIN	Coach	39A

Passenger Name	Ticket Number	Contact Number
SUZUKI/MARIYA MS	010-1233-5678	+819012345678

Purchase Description	Price
Fare	¥ 54,000
Passenger Facility Service Charge-Japan	¥ 2,000
Fee and Tax-USA	¥ 4,000
Fuel Surcharge	¥ 40,000
Number of Passengers	1
Total	¥ 100,000

When boarding AB Airlines operated flights, a passenger may carry a total of 10kg (22lbs) on board including one personal belonging, such as a shopping bag or a handbag, and one piece of luggage satisfying the following conditions: the sum of all three dimensions is not more than 115cm (45in) and each dimension is less than W55cm×H40cm×D25cm (W22in×H16in×D10in).

Unit 1　At the airport

Q1. How is the ticket issued?
　　A. By a travel agent
　　B. Through the web site
　　C. At the airline counter

Q2. How much did she pay besides her airfare?
　　A. She paid 100,000 yen.
　　B. She paid 46,000 yen.
　　C. She paid 46,001 yen.

Q3. Which personal items are accepted as carry-on baggage?
　　A. A duffle bag with an overall size of 110cm and a weight of 11kg
　　B. A musical instrument with dimensions of 60×30×25cm and a weight of 10kg
　　C. A garment bag with dimensions of 20×14×10in and a weight of 14lbs

Numbers

音声を聞き、書き取りなさい。

＜ Flight Numbers ＞
　　例： NH1122

(1) _____　(2) _____　(3) _____
(4) _____　(5) _____

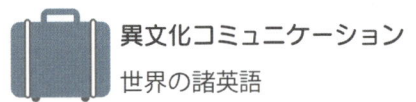

異文化コミュニケーション
世界の諸英語

　Inner Circle（内側の円）は、第一言語として英語を使っている、あるいは母語として英語を話している人々が暮らす国を表している。英国、アメリカ合衆国、オーストラリア、カナダ、ニュージーランドで人口は約3億2千万人から3億8千万人である。Outer Circle（外側の円）は多言語国家における政府の公式言語や第二外国語として英語を話す人たちが居住する国々を表わしている。旧英国植民地である、インド、ケニア、パキスタン、シンガポール等、あるいは米国に統治されていたフィリピンなどが含まれる。その人口は1億5千万人から3億人と推定される。Expanding Circle（拡張の円）は国際言語として英語を話す国である。日本もその中に含まれる。つまり、英語を使うのは、母語話者より非母語話者の方が圧倒的に多い。同時に英語は、非母語話者同士の共通言語として機能している。

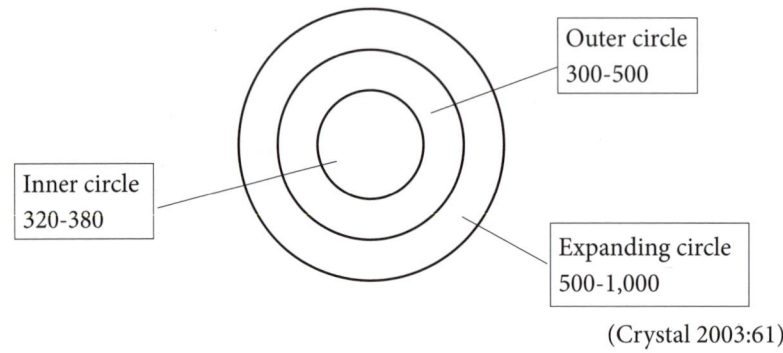

(Crystal 2003:61)

参考文献　David Crystal (2003). English as a global language (2nd Ed). Cambridge University Press.

Survival Activity
あなただったらどうする？
＜ケース1＞
空港までの道路が渋滞し、出発便チェックインの締切時刻に間に合いそうにない。
　このような場面に遭遇した時、あなたならどう対処するか考えてみよう。
　また、その時に使える英語表現を考え、ロールプレイをしてみよう。

Unit 2　On the plane

🌐 Vocabulary

次の語句の意味を下から選びなさい。

1. aisle   (   )   2. fasten   (   )
3. turbulence   (   )   4. headset   (   )
5. masterpiece   (   )   6. time zone   (   )
7. secure   (   )   8. underneath   (   )
9. expect   (   ) 10. device   (   )
11. compartment (   ) 12. upright   (   )
13. fleet   (   ) 14. including   (   )
15. feature   (   )

乱気流	…をしっかり締める	装置、道具	小物入れ	ヘッドフォン
通路	…を含めて	…の下に	…をしまい込む	…の特色を成す
時間帯	名作、傑作	…を予期する	保有航空機	まっすぐな

Comprehension Check 7

音声を聞き、正しい答えを選びなさい。

Scene 1 <On the plane ① >

(1) Her seat is located on the (right / left) side of the aisle.

(2) Somebody is (sitting in her seat / waiting for her).

Scene 2 <On the plane ② >

(1) She (will receive a new / has brought her own) headset.

(2) She feels (comfortable / a little cold).

Scene 3 <On the plane ③ >

(1) She chooses (fish / vegetarian) for her in-flight meal.

(2) She orders (coffee / soda).

Listening 8

音声を聞き、（　　　）を埋めなさい。

Ladies and gentlemen, welcome on board Flight AB123 with (①　　　　　) from Tokyo to New York JFK Airport. This is your captain, Jane, speaking. We are (②　　　　　) to be in the air in approximately five minutes. We ask you to (③　　　　　) your seatbelts at this time and secure all baggage underneath your seat or in the (④　　　　　) compartments. We also ask that your seats and table trays be in the (⑤　　　　　) position for take-off. Please turn off all personal electronic (⑥　　　　　), including laptops and mobile phones. We are also expecting a little turbulence after taking off. Please keep your seat belt fastened whenever you are in your seat. Thank you for choosing AB Airlines. Enjoy your flight.

Unit 2   On the plane

Pronunciation 9

次の飲料名を英語で書き、音声を聞いて発音しなさい。

コーヒー　　　　（　　　　　　　　）
カフェイン抜きコーヒー　（　　　　　　　　）
日本茶　　　　（　　　　　　）　牛乳　　　　（　　　　　　　　）
ミルクティー　（　　　　　　）　ココア　　　（　　　　　　　　）
オレンジジュース（　　　　　　）　ハーブティ　（　　　　　　　　）
炭酸水　　　　（　　　　　　）

Useful Expressions 10

ペアで練習しなさい。

1. (A) Do you have any aisle seats?
   (B) I'm afraid not.
2. (A) Do you have any extra blankets?
   (B) Unfortunately, they're all in use.
3. (A) Do you have any more headsets?
   (B) We sure do.
4. (A) Have you got red wine?
   (B) Of course. I'll bring it right away.

 Reading

次の文を読み、Q1〜Q3に答えなさい。

Many of the aircrafts in our international fleet feature on-demand entertainment systems, allowing you to relax and enjoy a variety of entertainment options during your in-flight experience.

Wreck-It Ralph	*The Godfather*	*Argo*
Duration: 1hr 41min Category: Animated Family Comedy Language: English, Spanish; Chinese subtitles Director: Rich Moore Voice: John C. Reilly, Jack McBrayer Ralph, a video game villain, wants to be a hero but his quest accidentally brings chaos to the whole arcade where he lives.	Duration: 2hrs 55min Category: Drama, Thriller Language: English, Italian, French Director: Francis Ford Coppola Stars: Marlon Brando, Al Pacino Francis Ford Coppola's masterpiece describes a chilling portrait of the rise and fall of a family in the New York Mafia.	Duration: 2hrs 00min Category: Drama, Thriller Language: English, German, Japanese Director: Ben Affleck Stars: Ben Affleck, Bryan Cranston, John Goodman Based on a true story of the life or death drama of the 1980 Iran hostage crisis. To get six US diplomats out, a CIA agent comes up with a plan.

Notes
villain 悪役　quest 冒険　arcade ゲームセンター
a chilling portrait 身震いするような描写
Iran hostage crisis イランで起きたアメリカ大使館員人質事件

Unit 2　On the plane

Q1. What is said about *The Godfather*?

 A. It is a story about an Italian family.

 B. The duration is about two hours.

 C. The audience can choose from three languages.

Q2. Which movie is based on facts?

 A. *Wreck-it Ralph*

 B. *The Godfather*

 C. *Argo*

Q3. Which movie can be recommended for children?

 A. *Wreck-it Ralph*

 B. *The Godfather*

 C. *Argo*

Numbers　　11

音声を聞き、書き取りなさい。

< Seat Numbers >

 例：10A

(1) _____　(2) _____　(3) _____

(4) _____　(5) _____

 Travel Tips
時差

　標準時は、英国にあるグリニッジ天文台を通る経度0度の子午線を基準にしている。これを世界時やグリニッジ標準時と呼び、経度0度を基準に、東西に12の標準時の時間帯（time zone）が設定されている。各時間帯は、地球の1日の回転360度を24時間で割った、経度15度の幅である。国土が広いアメリカはアラスカとハワイを除き4つの時間帯がある。ロシアには10の時間帯がある。また、日付変更線は太平洋の中央にあり、この線を西から東へ越えると日付は1日遅れ、逆に東から西に越えると日付が1日進む。

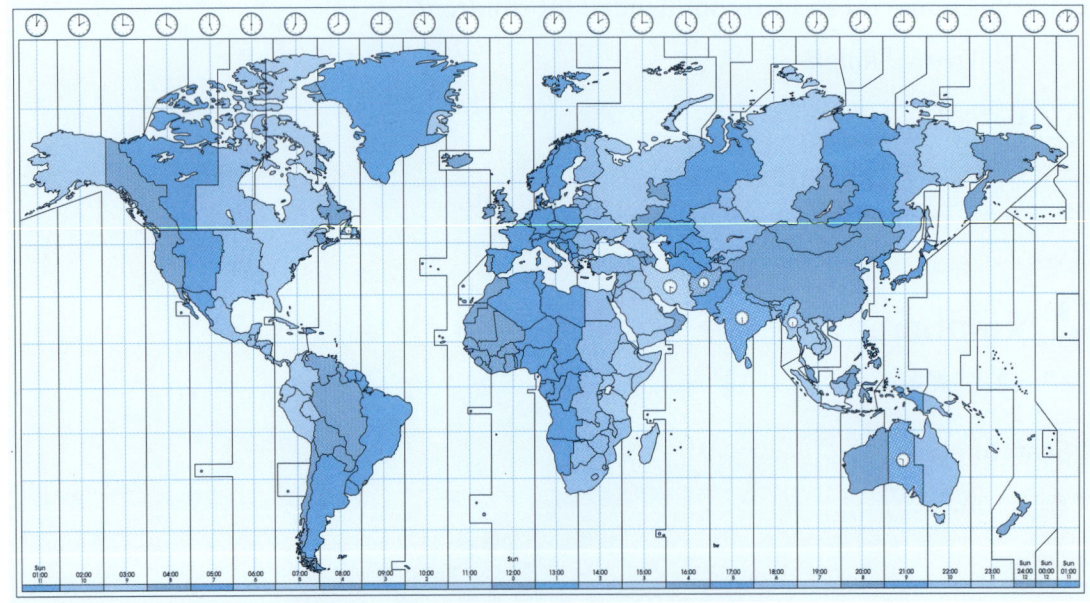

Survival Activity
あなただったらどうする？
＜ケース２＞
眠っている間に機内食が終わっていた。

このような場面に遭遇した時、あなたならどう対処するか考えてみよう。
また、その時に使える英語表現を考え、ロールプレイをしてみよう。

Unit 3　Arrival

🌐 Vocabulary

次の語句の意味を下から選びなさい。

1. immigration　(　　　)　　2. customs　(　　　)
3. lost and found　(　　　)　　4. fingerprint　(　　　)
5. proceed　(　　　)　　6. polka dot　(　　　)
7. baggage claim　(　　　)　　8. duration　(　　　)
9. be supposed to　(　　　)　　10. carousel　(　　　)
11. locate　(　　　)　　12. transportation　(　　　)
13. form　(　　　)　　14. delay　(　　　)
15. designated　(　　　)

税関	遺失物取扱所	継続時間	指紋	位置する
荷物受取所	指定された	入国管理	進む、進める	…する予定である
回転台	輸送手段	水玉模様	用紙	…を遅らせる

Comprehension Check 12

音声を聞き、正しい答えを選びなさい。

Scene 1 <At the immigration booth>

(1) She is going to stay for (four weeks / a week).

(2) First, she is required to place her (left / right) fingers on the scanner.

Scene 2 <At the lost-and-found office>

(1) Her baggage is hard with a (striped / polka-dot) belt.

(2) The officer asks her (the duration of her stay / her address) in the US.

Scene 3 <Ground transportation>

(1) She is going take (shared / public) transportation to Manhattan.

(2) The telephone is (on the wall / in front of the counter).

Listening 13

音声を聞き、(　　　) を埋めなさい。

Welcome to JFK International Airport. The baggage carousels are located on the (①　　　　) level of the (②　　　　　) terminal. After proceeding to the baggage claim (③　　　　　), please go to the (④　　　　　) carousel for your flight to claim your check-in baggage. Passengers from AB airlines flight 123 from Tokyo should please (⑤　　　　　) to baggage carousel number six to collect your baggage. (⑥　　　　　) are available at the area for your use. Also, please have your customs form ready for inspection.

Unit 3　Arrival

Pronunciation 14

次の色や柄の表現を英語で書き、音声を聞いて発音しなさい。

紺色	(	)	赤色	(	)
紫色	(	)	灰色	(	)
ベージュ	(	)	縞模様	(	)
格子縞	(	)	水玉模様	(	)
無地	(	)			

Useful Expressions 15

ペアで練習しなさい。

1. (A) I'm sorry? Would you repeat that more slowly?
   (B) Certainly.
2. (A) Excuse me? Would you say that again?
   (B) Sure.
3. (A) Pardon me? Could you write it out?
   (B) Sure, why not?
4. (A) I'm sorry, my English isn't very good.
   (B) It's no problem.

 **Reading**

次の文を読み、Q1～Q3に答えなさい。

Hotel Hop provides on-time, economical and safe shared-van transfers, door to door in both directions between Manhattan and JFK Airport, 24 hours a day, 7 days a week. We serve hotels, major terminals and corporate offices with modern, comfortable vans.
Fare: One way to Manhattan $16.00, round trip $31.00
Prices above are not including sales tax and tips.
Book online now!

www.hotelhop.com

GOGO Airport Shuttle Bus
Fast and Frequent
Your express ride to NYC
Daily departure from each terminal from 5:00 A.M. to midnight. Every 20-30 minutes.
JFK to Grand Central Station in Manhattan only $15.00.
We offer free shuttle van service from Grand Central Station to Times Square & Mid-town between 33rd and 63rd streets for GOGO Airport Shuttle Bus customers. Kids go free! Call toll free (855)123-4567. If you book online, you automatically save $2.

www.gogoairportshuttle.com

Unit 3 Arrival

Q1. For whom is the information intended?

   A. Commuters

   B. Arriving passengers

   C. Airport employees

Q2. How can the reader get a discount?

   A. Use a coupon

   B. Visit their website

   C. Pay in cash

Q3. What is indicated about Hotel Hop?

   A. It provides transfer service only to hotels.

   B. It is a private charter.

   C. It operates all year round.

 # Numbers 🎧 16

音声を聞き、書き取りなさい。

< Durations of Time >

　例： 2 hours, 45 minutes, 30 seconds

(1) _____　(2) _____　(3) _____
(4) _____　(5) _____

 **異文化コミュニケーション**
察しの文化

　日本のコミュニケーションスタイルは、できごとを取り巻く情報に依存する「高コンテキスト文化」である。既に共有している情報が多いことを前提としているため、言語で多くを語る必要がない。相手の考えを察することが望まれるのである。一方、アメリカや北ヨーロッパ等は情報の共有を前提とせず、言語によって自分の意志を明確に伝える「低コンテキスト文化」である。

　従って、異文化との接触現場では空気を読んで「やってくれる」「わかってくれる」ことを相手に期待して黙っていては何も解決しない。知りたいことや困っていることがあれば、順序立てて言語で表現することが重要である。後で不平不満、愚痴を言っても状況は改善しないし、かえって悪化することもある。明確に意見を述べ、問題があればその場で解決に結びつける努力をしよう。

　参考　ホール、E.T.（1979）『文化を超えて』TBS ブリタニカ

Survival Activity

あなただったらどうする？

＜ケース3＞

空港で預けたスーツケースが壊れていた。

このような場面に遭遇した時、あなたならどう対処するか考えてみよう。
また、その時に使える英語表現を考え、ロールプレイをしてみよう。

Unit 4　Checking in at the hotel

🌐 Vocabulary

次の語句の意味を下から選びなさい。

1. slot　　　　　　(　　　　　)　　2. grill　　　　　　(　　　　　)
3. safe　　　　　　(　　　　　)　　4. reserve　　　　 (　　　　　)
5. local　　　　　 (　　　　　)　　6. commonly　　　 (　　　　　)
7. complimentary (　　　　　)　　8. swipe　　　　　(　　　　　)
9. PIN　　　　　　(　　　　　)　 10. water pressure (　　　　　)
11. currency　　　 (　　　　　)　 12. detail　　　　　(　　　　　)
13. through　　　 (　　　　　)　 14. accept　　　　 (　　　　　)
15. following　　　(　　　　　)

次の	暗唱番号	…を予約する	…を受け入れる	水圧
細長い溝	概して	無料の	…を焼く	貨幣
現地の	…を通じて	…を読み取り機に通す	貴重品入れ	詳細

Comprehension Check 17

音声を聞き、正しい答えを選びなさい

Scene 1 <At the front desk ① >

(1) She is going to stay for (four / six) nights.

(2) She reserved the room through (a travel agent / a website).

Scene 2 <At the front desk ② >

(1) The breakfast hour ends at (10:00 a.m. / 10:30 a.m.) on weekdays.

(2) The guests (must / don't need to) show their room keys for the breakfast.

Scene 3 <At the front desk ③ >

(1) Her (credit card / card key) doesn't work.

(2) The clerk changes (her key / the program).

Listening 18

音声を聞き、(　　　) を埋めなさい。

A continental breakfast is a (①　　　　) meal, which usually includes cereal, fruit, bread, butter, jam, juice, tea and coffee. It is served commonly in Continental Europe. On the other hand, a typical American breakfast comprises eggs, bacon or sausage, cereal, baked foods such as donuts and muffins, coffee and tea, milk, and juice. A (②　　　　) English breakfast may consist of cooked dishes such as baked beans, porridge, boiled eggs, bacon, grilled fish, sausage, grilled or fried (③　　　　) or tomatoes. This is followed by (④　　　　), toasted bread and (⑤　　　　), tea and coffee. However, all of these can (⑥　　　　) from one part of the country to another.

Unit 4 Checking in at the hotel

 Pronunciation   19

次の食品名を英語で書き、音声を聞いて発音しなさい。

シリアル	(	)	パン	(	)
バターロール	(	)	ヨーグルト	(	)
トースト	(	)	マーガリン	(	)
バター	(	)	ホットケーキ	(	)
ベーグル	(	)			

Useful Expressions   20

ペアで練習しなさい。

1. (A) I'm having a problem with my room key.
   (B) I can't open the door with it.
2. (A) I'm having a problem with the safe.
   (B) I forgot my PIN number.
3. (A) I'm having a problem with the shower.
   (B) The water pressure is too low.
4. (A) I have a problem with the heater.
   (B) It doesn't get hot.

Reading

次の文を読み、Q1～Q3に答えなさい

Thank you! Your booking is now confirmed.

EHotelBooking.com

Booking Number	123 456 789
Name of the guest	Mariya Suzuki
Booking details	6 nights, 1 room

New York Hotel

Address: 243 60th Street, New York, NY 10019

Phone: +1 (212) 987 6543

e-mail:res@NYhotel.com

Check-in	March-12-2015 After 15:00
Check-out	March-18-2015 Before 12:00
Total room price	US$800

You will pay at the hotel in local currency (US$).

Tax (14.75%) not included

City Tax (US$14) not included

The guest room has an ultramodern interior, with two separate beds, a flat TV and free Wi-Fi.

Cancellation cost:

Until March -6- 2015 23:59 {New York} US$0

From March -7- 2015 00:00 {New York} US$200

Important information

Upon check-in, photo identification and credit card are required. This hotel accepts the following forms of payment: American Express, Visa, Master Card

Unit 4 Checking in at the hotel

Q1. What is this document?

   A. A ticket

   B. A confirmation

   C. A bill

Q2. What is indicated about the room?

   A. Its interior is very new.

   B. Its interior is traditional.

   C. It is spacious.

Q3. Which is said about the payment?

   A. The room costs eight hundred dollars plus two types of taxes.

   B. Guests are able to use any credit card.

   C. Guests are able to pay with Japanese yen.

 **Numbers** 21

音声を聞き、書き取りなさい。

< Dates >

例：5/26/2000（M/D/Y）

(1) _____　(2) _____　(3) _____
(4) _____　(5) _____

 **Travel Tips**
署名と名前

　欧米において「sign（サイン）をする」ということは、押印と同様の意味を持つ。もともと印鑑は古代メソポタミアに端を発し、中世ヨーロッパでは王侯・貴族の間で使われていた。しかし、近代になってからは諸外国で印鑑が使用されることは非常に稀であり、署名を用いる場合がほとんどである。海外旅行中における唯一の身分証明書であるパスポートの署名が漢字、旅行者小切手（トラベラーズチェック）の署名欄がローマ字になっていると、照合の際に問題となる。また、書類に署名をする際は、法的行為であると認識し、内容を理解した上で署名しよう。簡単に人にまねされないように工夫することも必要である。一方、name（名前）欄には署名ではなく、誰にでも読めるよう名前を print（活字で書く）ことが求められる。

Survival Activity
あなただったらどうする？
＜ケース４＞
予約した条件と違う部屋に案内された。

このような場面に遭遇した時、あなたならどう対処するか考えてみよう。
また、その時に使える英語表現を考え、ロールプレイをしてみよう。

Unit 5　Getting information and sightseeing

🌐 Vocabulary

次の語句の意味を下から選びなさい。

1. major　　　　(　　　　)　　2. block　　　　　(　　　　)
3. suggest　　　(　　　　)　　4. double-decker　(　　　　)
5. brochure　　 (　　　　)　　6. forecast　　　 (　　　　)
7. pleasant　　 (　　　　)　　8. work　　　　　(　　　　)
9. cover　　　 (　　　　)　　10. explore　　　 (　　　　)
11. floor plan　(　　　　)　　12. unlimited　　 (　　　　)
13. cathedral　 (　　　　)　　14. offer　　　　 (　　　　)
15. affordable　(　　　　)

一区画	快適な	主要な	2階建てバス	手ごろな価格の
作品	無制限の	（天気）予報	…を探索する	…にわたる
大教会堂	パンフレット	間取り図	…を提供する	…を提案する

 Comprehension Check   22

音声を聞き、正しい答えを選びなさい

Scene 1 <At the front desk>

(1) She wants to do some (shopping / sightseeing).

(2) She feels that is (affordable / too expensive).

Scene 2 <At the concierge desk ① >

(1) Make a (right / left) turn at the main entrance outside the hotel to get there.

(2) It's (difficult / easy) to find the place.

Scene 3 <At the concierge desk ② >

(1) It's going to be (windy / rainy) in the evening.

(2) The hotel has (one umbrella / many umbrellas).

Listening   23

音声を聞き、(　　　　) を埋めなさい。

This is the Metropolitan Museum of Art Information. The Museum has more than two (①　　　　) works of art covering (②　　　　) years of history, so it's a good idea to plan ahead. Seeing everything here could take a week. Before you begin exploring the museum, check the museum's floor plan for the locations of the major wings and collections. It's available at all the entrances. If you're hungry and want to eat inside the museum, there are several restaurants available. We are open from (③　　　　) a.m. to 5:30 p.m. from Tuesday to (④　　　　), 9:30 a.m. to 9:00 p.m. on Fridays and (⑤　　　　), and 9:30 a.m. to 5:30 p.m. on Sundays. We're closed on (⑥　　　　) and all state and federal holidays.

(www.metmuseum.org)

Unit 5 Getting information and sightseeing

🌐 Pronunciation   24

次の観光名所等を英語で書き、音声を聞いて発音しなさい。

自由の女神　　　(　　　　　　　)　　ロックフェラーセンター (　　　　　　　　　)

タイムズスクエア (　　　　　　　)　　ヤンキースタジアム　(　　　　　　　　　)

メトロポリタン美術館　(　　　　　　　　)

展望台　　　　(　　　　　　　)　　ブロードウェイ　(　　　　　　　　　)

国連本部　　　(　　　　　　　)　　リンカーンセンター (　　　　　　　　　)

🌐 Useful Expressions   25

ペアで練習しなさい。

1. (A) I'd like to see some of the major sights.
   (B) I'd suggest taking a bus tour.

2. (A) I'd like to go to the Empire State Building.
   (B) I'd suggest going there in the morning.

3. (A) I want to go shopping.
   (B) How about going to Nancy's Department Store?

4. (A) I want to see a musical.
   (B) How about going to the Times Square TKTS Booth?

33

 Reading

次の文を読み、Q1～Q3に答えなさい。

City Sightseeing NY

See New York from an open top double-decker bus! (48 Hours)

Frequent daily departures include a round trip ferry ticket to the Statue of Liberty, tickets to the observation deck of one of the magnificent buildings of the world, the Empire State Building, the Downtown Loop, the Uptown Loop, Brooklyn and a one-hour night tour. Stop at more than 50 places! Unlimited hop-on, hop-off! Buses are furnished with state-of-the art sound systems with various languages. You will also get a discount coupon for the biggest department store in Manhattan!
We've got the perfect tour for you.

Adult $75 Child (3-11) $55   Tickets valid for 48 hours

Add an extra day on the double-decker for only $12 more!
Offer only valid at the time of purchase.

Visit our website for more information: www.citysightseeingny.com or call toll free 1-800-234-5678

Q1. What is the purpose of the advertisement?

　　A. To announce an event

　　B. To advertise a tour

　　C. To advertise a new bus

Q2. What is mentioned in the advertisement?

　　A. Visiting the Empire State Building is included.

　　B. Tickets for three-year-old children are free of charge.

　　C. An audio guide is available.

Q3. What should people do if they want more details?

　　A. Visit the Website

　　B. Ask at the information desk

　　C. Send an E-mail

Numbers　　　26

音声を聞き、書き取りなさい。

＜ Times 1 ＞

　　例： 12:00

(1) _____　(2) _____　(3) _____
(4) _____　(5) _____

Travel Tips
摂氏と華氏

　華氏はドイツ人物理学者の Gabriel Daniel Fahrenheit 氏が 1724 年に考案した温度目盛で 212 度を沸点、32 度を水の凝固点としている。米国では華氏が一般的に使われており、英国でも非公式な場では使用されている。日本語の「華氏」は Fahrenheit の中国語に由来する。一方、スエーデンの天文学者 Anders Celsius 氏が 1742 年に考案した摂氏は氷の凝固点を 0 度、沸点を 100 度としている。考案者の名前から Celsius、あるいは Centigrade と呼ばれている。華氏と摂氏の計算式は以下である。天気予報の際にまごつかないよう、例えば、「華氏 70 度は摂氏 21 度ほど」と覚えておくとよい。

$$F=(C \times 9 \div 5) + 32$$
$$C=(F - 32) \times 5 \div 9$$

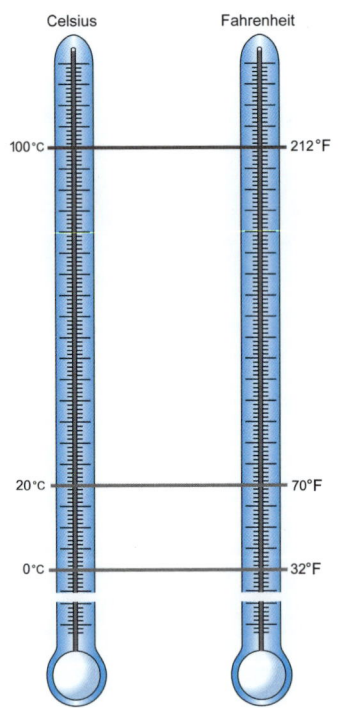

Survival Activity
あなただったらどうする？
＜ケース 5＞
ホテルの周辺で食事をしたいのだが、どのレストランが良いのかわからない。
　このような場面に遭遇した時、あなたならどう対処するか考えてみよう。
　また、その時に使える英語表現を考え、ロールプレイをしてみよう。

Unit 6　Ordering fast food

Vocabulary

次の語句の意味を下から選びなさい。

1. order　　　　　(　　　　　)　　2. wheat　　　　(　　　　　)
3. change　　　　(　　　　　)　　4. regular　　　　(　　　　　)
5. crispy　　　　 (　　　　　)　　6. top　　　　　　(　　　　　)
7. recommend　　(　　　　　)　　8. convenient　　(　　　　　)
9. criticize　　　 (　　　　　)　　10. conscious　　 (　　　　　)
11. choose　　　 (　　　　　)　　12. payment　　　(　　　　　)
13. favorite　　　(　　　　　)　　14. accompany　　(　　　　　)
15. flavor　　　　(　　　　　)

便利な	カリカリした	…を選ぶ	…を注文する	小麦
味	…の上に乗せる	支払い	…を非難する	大好きな
おつり	…に添える	普通の	…に敏感な	…を勧める

Comprehension Check 🎧 27

音声を聞き、正しい答えを選びなさい。

Scene 1 <At the sandwich shop>

(1) She orders a (regular / small) size drink.

(2) She is going to (eat at the shop / take the food out).

Scene 2 <At the fast food restaurant>

(1) She orders a (mixed berry / strawberry) frozen yogurt.

(2) Her total payment is ($12.50 / $11.50).

Scene 3 <At the burger shop>

(1) The sales person recommends her the (original / mustard) sauce.

(2) The hamburger has been topped with (tomato / lettuce).

Listening 🎧 28

音声を聞き、(　　　) を埋めなさい。

Fast food is (①　　　　　), convenient and for many of us, it tastes good. But having too much fast food can lead to health problems. Fast food restaurants are often criticized by health conscious people because of their (②　　　　　) menus. A typical meal at a burger shop consists of a sandwich, a medium fries, and a regular-size drink, all of which can add up to 1400 calories. So let's make healthier choices at fast food restaurants. Order (③　　　　　) with more vegetables and choose leaner meats. A better (④　　　　　) would be a (⑤　　　　　) burger which is about three hundred calories, a small (⑥　　　　　) and a diet coke, which makes about five hundred calories.

Unit 6　Ordering fast food

🌐 Pronunciation　　🎧 29

次の飲食物等を英語で書き、音声を聞いて発音しなさい。

ポテトフライ	(　　　　)	ホットドッグ	(　　　　　　)
アップルパイ	(　　　　)	ケチャップ	(　　　　　　)
マヨネーズ	(　　　　)	アイスティー	(　　　　　　)
アイスクリーム	(　　　　)	バニラ	(　　　　　　)
サンドイッチ	(　　　　)		

🌐 Useful Expressions　　🎧 30

ペアで練習しなさい。

1. (A) What would you like to drink?
   (B) Let me see…
2. (A) We have our own original mayonnaise.
   (B) Okay, let me try it.
3. (A) What's the price?
   (B) Let me check.
4. (A) Can you wait a moment?
   (B) Certainly. Let me know when you're ready.

Reading

次の文を読み、Q1～Q3に答えなさい。

Bitin' Bagels

Breakfast and Lunch are Served All Day!!

Choose your favorite bagel:

Plain / Sesame / Poppy / Cinnamon / Raisin / Onion / Wheat / Blueberry

All Sandwiches are served with pickles

(1/2 portion price)

Lunch (11:00-15:00)

Turkey Bacon Bagel

Sliced turkey, lettuce, tomato, mayo or mustard, and cheddar cheese on your choice of bagel… 5.55 (3.00)

Chicken Bacon Bagel

Sliced chicken grilled with bacon, and topped with lettuce, tomato, onions and your choice of mayo or mustard on your choice of bagel… 5.55 (3.00)

Vegetarian Bagel

Veggie cream cheese, avocado, tomato & melted cheese served open faced on your choice of bagel… 4.35 (2.75)

Grilled Cheese Bagel

A bagel of your choice grilled with butter and melted cheddar cheese… 3.50 (2.00)

Drinks

Coffee… 3.50	Smoothies… 3.50	Soda… 1.50 (1.00)
Mocha	Blueberry	Coke
Caramel Latte	Mango	Diet Coke
Vanilla Latte	Strawberry	Perrier

Q1. Which meal would you order if you didn't like cheese?

    A. A turkey bacon bagel

    B. A chicken bacon bagel

    C. A vegetarian bagel

Q2. Which statement is correct according to the menu?

    A. Sandwiches are always accompanied by pickles.

    B. You can choose your favorite bagel from five flavors.

    C. They serve only at lunch time.

Q3. How much is the total price for a chicken bagel and a smoothie?

    A. $7.00

    B. $10.00

    C. $9.05

Numbers

CD 31

音声を聞き、書き取りなさい。

< Fractions >

例：1/2

(1) _____ (2) _____ (3) _____
(4) _____ (5) _____

異文化コミュニケーション
選択肢と多様性

　アメリカではファーストフードを注文する際にその選択肢の多さにしばしば驚かされる。パンの種類、はさむ野菜の種類、チーズは何が良いか、量はどのくらいか、ケチャップは、マスタードは・・・と、簡単に注文できるはずのファーストフードの注文がなかなか難しい。コーヒーを注文する際にも regular（通常の）か decaf（カフェイン抜きの）か、サイズは・・・と多くの選択肢が用意されている。これは米国の多様性を反映している。人はそれぞれ異なる。当然食事の好みも異なり、多くの選択肢を提供することが良いサービスの1つであると考えられている。お客は臆することなく細かく希望を伝える。慣れるまではメニューをじっくり読んでから注文しよう。

Survival Activity

あなただったらどうする？

＜ケース6＞

ハンバーガーショップでテーブルに行く途中、ジュースを床にこぼしてしまった。

このような場面に遭遇した時、あなたならどう対処するか考えてみよう。
また、その時に使える英語表現を考え、ロールプレイをしてみよう。

Unit 7　Going to the theater

Vocabulary

次の語句の意味を下から選びなさい。

1. rear	( )	2. chart	( )
3. production	( )	4. remind	( )
5. prohibit	( )	6. strictly	( )
7. budget	( )	8. follow	( )
9. performance	( )	10. intermission	( )
11. courtesy	( )	12. matinée	( )
13. odd	( )	14. even	( )
15. auditorium	( )		

奇数	偶数	観客席	作品	演技、演奏
礼儀作法	絶対に	休憩	予算	後方の
表	…を思い出させる	…を禁止する	昼の公演	…について来る、行く

Comprehension Check 🎧 32

音声を聞き、正しい答えを選びなさい。

Scene 1 <At the tourist information counter>

(1) Same-day tickets may be (available / sold out).

(2) Buying discount tickets usually takes (a couple of hours / a half hour).

Scene 2 <At the box office>

(1) There are tickets ranging from ($26 to $122 / $36 to $122) available.

(2) The seats are (next to each other / separated).

Scene 3 <With the usher>

(1) The length of the performance is more than (two / three) hours.

(2) The audience can get (drinks / food) during the intermission.

Listening 🎧 33

音声を聞き、(　　　) を埋めなさい。

Good evening ladies and gentlemen. Welcome to *Majestic Theatre* and tonight's (①　　　　) of *The Phantom of the Opera*, which won a Tony Award for Best Musical and now is the longest-(②　　　　) show in Broadway history. The show will begin in a few (③　　　　). At this time we would like to remind you to put your (④　　　　), and any other devices that make (⑤　　　　) in silent mode as a courtesy to the actors on stage and your fellow (⑥　　　　) members. Recordings and photos of any kind are strictly prohibited by copyright law. Thank you very much and enjoy the show.

Unit 7　Going to the theater

🔵 Pronunciation　　　🎧 34

次の国名・都市名を英語で書き、音声を聞いて発音しなさい。

ドイツ	(	)	イタリア	(	)
ベネチア	(	)	ローマ	(	)
ギリシャ	(	)	アテネ	(	)
スイス	(	)	ベルギー	(	)
オランダ	(	)			

🔵 Useful Expressions　　　🎧 35

ペアで練習しなさい

1. (A) If you have time, you could visit the Statue of Liberty.
   (B) Sounds nice.
2. (A) If you visit New York, go see a musical.
   (B) Good idea.
3. (A) If you don't mind, I'll go with you.
   (B) Not at all. Let's go.
4. (A) If you stop by Times Square, you can go to the TKTS for a discount ticket.
   (B) Great.

Reading

チケットと座席表を読み、Q1〜Q3に答えなさい。

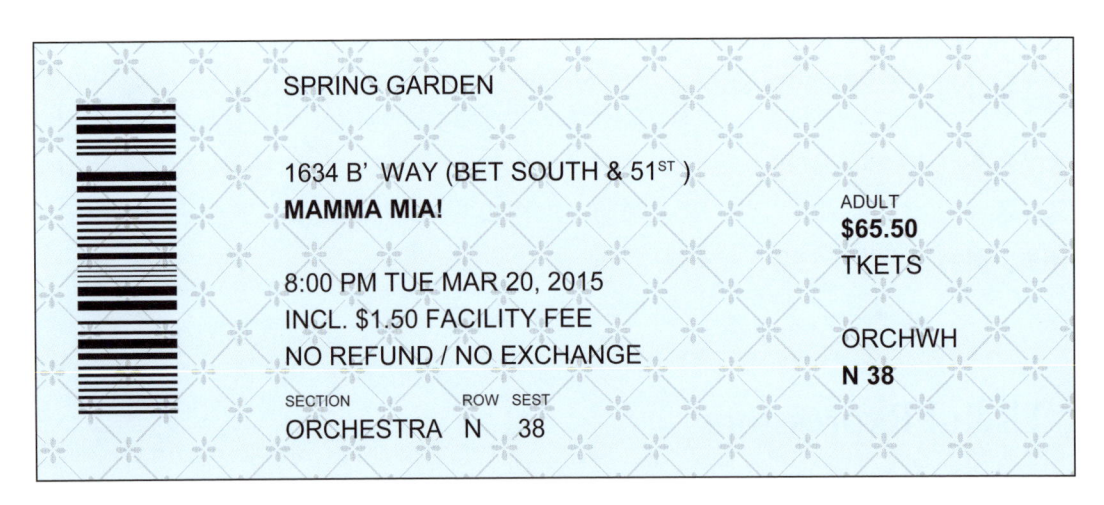

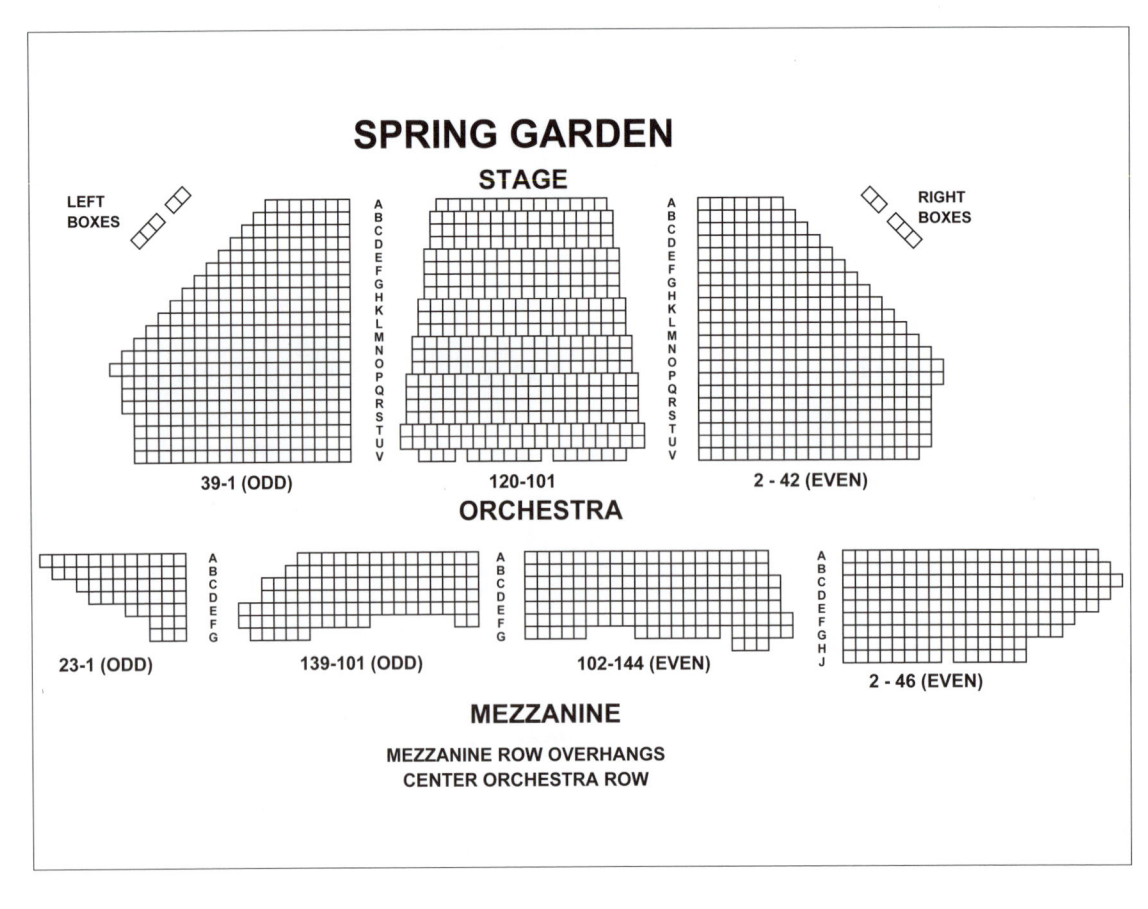

SPRING GARDEN

1634 B' WAY (BET SOUTH & 51ST)
MAMMA MIA!

8:00 PM TUE MAR 20, 2015
INCL. $1.50 FACILITY FEE
NO REFUND / NO EXCHANGE

ADULT
$65.50
TKETS

ORCHWH
N 38

SECTION   ROW   SEST
ORCHESTRA   N   38

SPRING GARDEN

STAGE

LEFT BOXES   RIGHT BOXES

39-1 (ODD)   120-101   2 - 42 (EVEN)

ORCHESTRA

23-1 (ODD)   139-101 (ODD)   102-144 (EVEN)   2 - 46 (EVEN)

MEZZANINE

MEZZANINE ROW OVERHANGS
CENTER ORCHESTRA ROW

Unit 7 Going to the theater

Q1. How much is the ticket?

   A. $65.50

   B. $64.00

   C. $38.00

Q2. Where is the seat on the ticket?

   A. Around the middle of the auditorium

   B. The right side of the auditorium

   C. The rear section of the auditorium

Q3. Which information is not indicated on the ticket?

   A. The time the show begins

   B. The theater's location

   C. The name of the producer

Numbers

CD 36

音声を聞き、書き取りなさい。

< Prices 1 >

例：$110

(1) _____ (2) _____ (3) _____
(4) _____ (5) _____

異文化コミュニケーション
番号

　北米だけでなく、ヨーロッパでも大きな劇場などで座席が連続番号ではなく、奇数側と偶数側に配列が分かれていることがある。ステージに向かって中心より左側が奇数、右側が偶数である。また、国際的に広く使用されている住所表示は、通りの名前と、その通りに沿って順に付けられた建物番号で表示されている。道の片側が偶数なら反対側は奇数番号である。区域に名前と番号が付けられる街区方式を採用している日本とは異なる。さらに、欧米の客室数の多いホテルでは廊下をはさんで、部屋番号が偶数側と奇数側に分かれている場合がある。

Survival Activity

あなただったらどうする？

＜ケース 7 ＞

劇場で開演を待っている間、隣の席の人が話しかけてきた。

このような場面に遭遇した時、あなたならどう対処するか考えてみよう。
また、その時に使える英語表現を考え、ロールプレイをしてみよう。

Unit 8　At the restaurant

Vocabulary

次の語句の意味を下から選びなさい。

1. appetizer　　（　　　）　　2. entrée　　（　　　）
3. check　　　　（　　　）　　4. server　　（　　　）
5. diner　　　　（　　　）　　6. tap water　（　　　）
7. facility　　　（　　　）　　8. choice　　（　　　）
9. whip　　　　（　　　）　　10. gratuity　（　　　）
11. duplicate　　（　　　）　　12. due　　　（　　　）
13. credit　　　（　　　）　　14. occupy　　（　　　）
15. folks　　　　（　　　）

選択肢	施設	給仕	水道水	食事をする人
主菜	カードなどで支払う	…を泡立てる	心付け、チップ	支払うべき金額
写し	前菜	…を占める	勘定書き	みなさん

Comprehension Check CD 37

音声を聞き、正しい答えを選びなさい。

Scene 1. <At the entrance>

(1) A table by the window is (available / occupied).

(2) The receptionist will (take the order / send a server).

Scene 2 <Ordering food>

(1) They order (the same / different) drinks.

(2) The restaurant provides (faster / regular) service.

Scene 3 <Paying>

(1) The service charge is (included in / excluded from) the check.

(2) They charge for (two glasses / one glass) of lemonade.

Listening CD 38

音声を聞き、(　　　) を埋めなさい。

We have three wonderful (①　　　　　) for you tonight. First, there's grilled Alaskan king (②　　　　　) with olive and lemon sauce, served with wild rice and vegetables. We also have a 16-ounce sirloin steak that's cooked to order and served with grilled onions and your choice of potato or (③　　　　　). Lastly, today's pasta is (④　　　　　) fettuccine with flaked salmon in a white cream sauce and comes with a Caesar salad. You can also (⑤　　　　　) a dessert. We have milk chocolate mousse with macadamia cookies, a tropical fruit plate with passion fruit, mango, and mint. And of course we have traditional New York cheese cake with whipped cream. Coffee or tea is included in all (⑥　　　　　).

Unit 8　At the restaurant

🔵 Pronunciation　　🎧 39

次の食品・食材を英語で書き、音声を聞いて発音しなさい。

サラダ	(　　　　　)	オリーブオイル	(　　　　　)
キャベツ	(　　　　　)	子牛肉	(　　　　　)
ステーキ	(　　　　　)	オムレツ	(　　　　　)
ピザ	(　　　　　)	シーチキン	(　　　　　)
マカロニ	(　　　　　)		

🔵 Useful Expressions　　🎧 40

ペアで練習しなさい。

1. (A) What would you like to drink?
   (B) I'll have a glass of red wine.
2. (A) What would you like to start with?
   (B) We'll start with an appetizer
3. (A) Our special today is roast chicken.
   (B) Okay, I'll have that.
4. (A) Anything else?
   (B) Yes. We'll have some dessert.

Reading

次の文を読み、Q1～Q3に答えなさい。

NELLO'S STEAK HOUSE

53 W. 42st. ST. NEW YORK NY 10021

24. MAR. 2015

CHECK # 1996112-2

Table # 9 Server: Anny

DUPLICATE

1 SODA	$2.00
2 GLASSES OF WINE	$8.00
1 JUMBO SHRIMP COCKTAIL	$16.00
1 CLAM CHOWDER NEW ENGLAND STYLE	$8.00
1 BALSAMIC GREEN BEAN SALAD	$9.00
1 8oz BEEF TENDERLOIN	$25.00
1 HALF SIZE FILLET MIGNON	$15.00
1 SPAGHETTI WITH TOMATO SAUCE	$15.00
2 COFFEES	$0.00
1 TEA	$0.00
SUBTOTAL	$98.00
SALES TAX	$8.69
18% SERVICE CHARGE	$17.67

TOTAL DUE $124.36

Thank you for dining with us.

We are open all year round except Jan.1st.

Unit 8　At the restaurant

Q1. How many people most likely dined together?

　　A. Two

　　B. Three

　　C. Four

Q2. What is complimentary on the house?

　　A. Soft drinks

　　B. Any beverage

　　C. Tea and coffee

Q3. What is mentioned on the bill?

　　A. The restaurant may offer a vegetarian menu.

　　B. The restaurant offers brunch.

　　C. The restaurant is open 365 days.

🎧 Numbers 　　　　　　　🎧 41

音声を聞き、書き取りなさい。

< Prices 2 >

　　例： $50.25

(1) _____　(2) _____　(3) _____
(4) _____　(5) _____

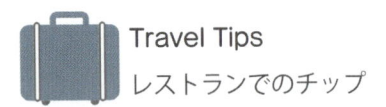

Travel Tips
レストランでのチップ

　チップの額は地域、レストランの質やサービスの質などによって異なり、その額は個人に任せられる。しかし、米国ではチップはほとんど「義務」として考えられている。もしチップを置かずに店を出れば、理由の説明を求められるかもしれない。（日本とは異なり、テーブルごとに担当者が決まっている。）多くのアメリカ人は税金前の合計に 15%から 20%を上乗せしたり「sales tax（消費税）の 2 倍」の金額をチップとして置く。観光客が多い場所では請求書に既に 20%ほどが加算されていることがある。欧州では、チップはそれほど厳格ではない。クレジットカードで支払う際には、チップの額と合計金額を支払い者が書き入れるようになっていることに注意しよう。

Survival Activity

あなただったらどうする？
＜ケース 8 ＞
レストランで注文した食事がなかなか出てこない。
このような場面に遭遇した時、あなたならどう対処するか考えてみよう。
また、その時に使える英語表現を考え、ロールプレイをしてみよう。

Unit 9　Shopping

Vocabulary

次の語句の意味を下から選びなさい。

1. pleased　　　(　　　)
2. enormous　　　(　　　)
3. terminal　　　(　　　)
4. transaction　　　(　　　)
5. refund　　　(　　　)
6. hesitate　　　(　　　)
7. anniversary　　　(　　　)
8. extra　　　(　　　)
9. unbelievable　　　(　　　)
10. eager　　　(　　　)
11. souvenir　　　(　　　)
12. equivalent　　　(　　　)
13. commemorate　(　　　)
14. surrender　　　(　　　)
15. expiration　　　(　　　)

端末	…に等しい	…を渡す	喜んでいる	巨大な
返金	余分な	信じられない	ためらう	…周年
土産	取り引き	記念する	熱心な	期限切れ

Comprehension Check 42

音声を聞き、正しい答えを選びなさい。

Scene 1 <At the shop>

(1) She wears American size (two or four / nine).

(2) The parka costs ($69 / $39).

Scene 2 <With the cashier>

(1) She is paying (with a credit card / in cash).

(2) She has (an extra / only one) card.

Scene 3 <At customer service>

(1) The sweater she bought is too (expensive / large).

(2) She'll (get a refund / exchange the item).

Listening 43

音声を聞き、(   ) を埋めなさい。

Attention World Hyper Market, we are pleased to announce that today is the first day of our week-long (①   ) to commemorate our 30th (②   ) since opening. Each day of the week, we'll be offering an unbelievable discount on a large number of different items for (③   ) customers, and an (④   ) 20% discount for our VIP cardholders. Please check our VIP customer lounge for more details. If you have any questions, please do not (⑤   ) to ask one of our sales (⑥   ) who are eager to answer all your questions and assist you in any way. Thank you for shopping at World Hyper Market!

Unit 9 Shopping

🔵 Pronunciation   44

次の語句を英語で書き、音声を聞いて発音しなさい。

デパート	(	)	トイレ	(	)
レジ係	(	)	値札	(	)
紙袋	(	)	ラベル	(	)
レジ袋	(	)	買い物かご	(	)
レシート	(	)			

🔵 Useful Expressions   45

ペアで練習しなさい。

1. (A) May I help you?

   (B) I'm just looking around.

2. (A) How can I help you?

   (B) Can I try these on?

3. (A) What are you looking for?

   (B) I'm looking for souvenirs for my friends.

4. (A) Are you looking for something in particular?

   (B) Nothing special.

Reading

次の広告を読み、Q1～Q3に答えなさい。

Mart Mall

NEW YORK SHOPPING MADE EASY!

The fun place to be in NYC!

DOZENS OF STORES ALL IN ONE PLACE

Mart Mall—just south of Times Square and close to the Empire State Building—is home to an enormous selection of the hottest shops with an enormous selection of fashion items, products for family and home, souvenirs and much more. Enjoy special savings during your visit with the coupons below!

Only at **Mart Mall**

valid through the end of the year

Save $5

On your purchase of $30 or more

Offer available in stores only. Excludes food, last sale items, gift cards, phone orders, special orders, assembly fees, delivery fees and shipping & handling. One coupon per customer. Not valid with any other transaction offer or on prior purchases. Must be surrendered at time of purchase. Only original coupons accepted.

1345 Broadway Manhattan   www.martmallNY.com   (212) 200-5678

Unit 9 Shopping

Q1. What is being advertised?

   A. A shopping mall

   B. A department store

   C. A supermarket

Q2. How can shoppers use the coupon?

   A. Visiting the store

   B. Making a purchase over $30

   C. Answering the quiz

Q3. For what is the coupon not valid?

   A. Interior goods

   B. Women's clothes

   C. Delivery fees

Numbers

CD 46

音声を聞き、書き取りなさい。

< Phone Numbers >

例： 555-2079

(1) _____   (2) _____   (3) _____
(4) _____   (5) _____

異文化コミュニケーション
店でのあいさつ

　アメリカで店に入ると店員が Hi, how are you doing? と声をかけてくることが多い。単なる挨拶なので特に手伝いが必要でなければ Hi, good などと答えればよい。May I help you? と聞かれた場合はきちんと返事をすることが期待される。日本では店員に「いらっしゃいませ」と声をかけられても挨拶を返さず、出て行く際も無言の場合がしばしばあるが、欧米人にはとても不思議な光景に見えるらしい。日本ではサービス提供者と受給者の間に上下関係が存在するが、欧米では二者の関係は基本的に対等である。挨拶はその対等なコミュニケーションの第一歩であり、人間関係の潤滑油である。店員に Thank you と言われれば返答は Thank you（You are welcome ではない）、Have a nice day! と言われれば、You, too 等と返そう。

Survival Activity
あなただったらどうする？
＜ケース 9 ＞

　買い物の際に受け取った、レシートを見ると、実際に購入した品物の数より1つ多く請求されていた。

　　このような場面に遭遇した時、あなたならどう対処するか考えてみよう。
　　また、その時に使える英語表現を考え、ロールプレイをしてみよう。

Unit 10　Lost and found

Vocabulary

次の語句の意味を下から選びなさい。

1. improve　　　(　　　　　)　　2. security　　　(　　　　　)
3. notice　　　(　　　　　)　　4. immediately　　(　　　　　)
5. describe　　　(　　　　　)　　6. officer　　　(　　　　　)
7. property　　　(　　　　　)　　8. representative　(　　　　　)
9. serial　　　(　　　　　)　　10. turn in　　　(　　　　　)
11. zip　　　(　　　　　)　　12. purse　　　(　　　　　)
13. extension　　(　　　　　)　　14. otherwise　　(　　　　　)
15. hours of operation　(　　　　　)

直ちに	…の特徴を述べる	営業時間	代理人	郵便番号
所有物	…を改善する	係官	…に気が付く	ポーチ
通しの	…を届ける	内線番号	警備	さもなければ

Comprehension Check 47

音声を聞き、正しい答えを選びなさい。

Scene 1 <On the phone>

(1) She lost her (glasses / PC case).

(2) Drivers turn in (few / many) pairs of glasses to the office.

Scene 2 <With the security officer ① >

(1) She lost her (bag / passport).

(2) She had put her property (on the chair / on the table).

Scene 3 <With the security officer ② >

(1) The security officer recommends that she stop her (telephone number / credit card).

(2) She's required to (complete / hold) the form.

Listening 48

音声を聞き、(　　　)を埋めなさい。

Thank you for calling Century Shopping (① 　　　　). In order to improve our services, the (② 　　　　) may be recorded. If you know the extension of the person you wish to reach, you may dial it at any time. Otherwise, please choose from one of the following options. To reach customer service, press 1. Press 2 if you want to talk to a sales representative, press 3 if you want company information such as hours of (③ 　　　　) and location. Press 4 for lost and found. Press 5 to (④ 　　　　) the message. If you don't know the number, (⑤ 　　　　) on the line. We'll connect you to an (⑥ 　　　　). The first available operator will be with you shortly.

Unit 10 Lost and found

Pronunciation   CD 49

次の語句を英語で書き、音声を聞いて発音しなさい。

財布　　　　（　　　　　　　）　　小銭入れ　　（　　　　　　　　）
携帯電話　　（　　　　　　　）　　折りたたみ傘（　　　　　　　　）
キーホルダー（　　　　　　　）　　文具　　　　（　　　　　　　　）
充電器　　　（　　　　　　　）　　手帳　　　　（　　　　　　　　）
腕時計　　　（　　　　　　　）

Useful Expressions   CD 50

ペアで練習しなさい。

1. (A) You should report it to the police office.
   (B) Oh, really?

2. (A) Should I call the security officer?
   (B) Yes, you should.

3. (A) You'd better leave now, or you'll be late.
   (B) Right, I'll leave shortly.

4. (A) You'd better not go to a place like that.
   (B) Okay, I understand.

Reading

次のレポートを読み、Q１～Q３に答えなさい。

LOST-PROPERTY REPORT　　　　　　　　　Date <u>Apr. 10, 2015</u>

REPORT NUMBER: _____

Call <u>(213) 123-4567</u> and ask for a "lost property" report number. If this number is not filled in, your report will not be recorded by the department.

NAME OF PERSON OWNING PROPERTY

NAME <u>Mariya Suzuki</u>

STREET <u>New York Hotel, 243, 60th Street, New York, NY</u>

SUITE/APT <u>Room #203</u>

CITY/ST/ZIP <u>NEW YORK/ NY/ 10019</u>

TELEPHONE <u>(212) 987-6543</u>

Location of Loss <u>345 W. 58th Street</u>　Zip <u>10019</u>

Type of location <u>Shopping Mall</u>

Date property last seen <u>Apr. 10, 2015</u>　Time <u>9:00</u>　(AM) or PM (circle one)

Date property discovered missing <u>Apr. 10, 2015</u>　Time <u>10:00</u>　(AM) or PM (circle one)

PERSON MAKING REPORT (If different from owner)

Contact phone #

Name: _____

Home address #

Street: _____ City: _____ State: _____ Zip: _____)

PROPERTY

QTY	DESCRIPTION (Serial numbers if available)	COST EACH	COST TTL
1	wallet	$150	$150
1	mobile phone	$299	$299
		Total loss	**$ 449**

Unit 10 Lost and found

Q1. When did the person lose her belongings?

   A. One day before

   B. In the morning

   C. In the afternoon

Q2. How many items has the person lost?

   A. One item

   B. Two items

   C. Three items

Q3. What is the person required to do to get the report number?

   A. Must fill out the form

   B. Must go to the office

   C. Must call a certain telephone number

I found this.

Numbers 🎧 CD 51

音声を聞き、書き取りなさい。

< Street Names >

例：2nd Street

(1) _____ (2) _____ (3) _____
(4) _____ (5) _____

Travel Tips
クレジットカード

　海外旅行に出かける際にはクレジットカードを必ず持参しよう。特に北米では現金よりもカードでの支払いが一般的で、金額にかかわらずほとんどの場所においてカードでの支払いが可能である。クレジットカードは一種の支払い能力証明の役割も果たしている。国際的に広く通用するカードを用意しよう。また、使用限度額を確認するとともに、盗難や紛失に備えてクレジットカード番号と発行会社の緊急連絡先を控えておくことを忘れてはならない。旅行者小切手は現金とは異なり紛失時に再発行可能である点が有利だが、使用時にパスポートなどの身分証明書の提示を求められることがある。

Survival Activity
あなただったらどうする？
<ケース 10>
旅行中に道端で人とぶつかって、気が付いた時にはバックの中の財布がなかった。
　　このような場面に遭遇した時、あなたならどう対処するか考えてみよう。
　　また、その時に使える英語表現を考え、ロールプレイをしてみよう。

Unit 11　Using public transportation

🌐 Vocabulary

次の語句の意味を下から選びなさい。

1. round trip   (   )   2. depend on   (   )
3. vary   (   )   4. transfer   (   )
5. temporary   (   )   6. suspension   (   )
7. outage   (   )   8. resume   (   )
9. cause   (   )   10. calmly   (   )
11. be subject to (   )   12. visibility   (   )
13. severe   (   )   14. cooperation   (   )
15. adjust   (   )

（一時的）不通	…によって決まる	落ち着いて	（天候等が）厳しい	異なる
停電	…を再開する	…しやすい	視界	乗換券
往復	…を引き起こす	協力	調整する	一時的な

Comprehension　　　CD 52

音声を聞き、正しい答えを選びなさい。

Scene 1　<At the station ① >

(1) The 1 Line on the subway is marked in (red / yellow) on the map.

(2) After getting off the train, take a (bus / boat).

Scene 2　<With the bus driver>

(1) Each ride costs ($2.50 / $2.75) if you pay in cash.

(2) Passengers are not able to pay by (coins / bills).

Scene 3　<At the station ② >

(1) She asks about (the price / the duration) of the trip.

(2) She wants to come back (on the same day / on another day).

Listening　　　CD 53

音声を聞き、(　　　) を埋めなさい。

Attention all passengers, an important (① 　　　) will follow. We are having a temporary suspension of service because of an electric outage caused by heavy (② 　　　) from a couple days before. We expect to resume service shortly but it may take longer. We (③ 　　　) for any inconvenience this may cause. We must ask all (④ 　　　) to calmly and quietly walk from the subway platform towards (⑤ 　　　) 1 through 5. Subway attendants will assist your transfer to a bus that will take you to your original (⑥ 　　　). Thank you for your cooperation.

Unit 11 Using public transportation

🔵 Pronunciation 　🔘 54

次の語句を英語で書き、音声を聞いて発音しなさい。

ルート	(	)	プラットホーム	(	)
自動販売機	(	)	フェリー	(	)
バイク	(	)	リムジン	(	)
往復	(	)	片道	(	)
釣銭	(	)			

🔵 Useful Expressions 　🔘 55

ペアで練習しなさい。

1. (A) Is a round trip cheaper?

    (B) Yes, it is. It's much cheaper.

2. (A) Is there a train leaving later?

    (B) No, this is the last one.

3. (A) Are trains more comfortable than planes?

    (B) I think so, but it depends on the person.

4. (A) Is traveling by train less expensive than by plane?

    (B) Generally, yes.

Reading

次の掲示を読み、Q1〜Q3に答えなさい。

The Staten Island Ferry
Weekday Schedule

Staten Island Ferry Departures

Depart Manhattan Whitehall Terminal

Doesn't Operate Monday Mornings

AM	PM
12:00	12:00
every 30 minutes	every 30 minutes
6:30	4:00
6:50	every 15 minutes
7:10	7:00
7:30	7:20
every 15 minutes	7:40
9:30	8:00
every 30 minutes	every 30 minutes

Caution

All schedules are subject to change without notice. Please check this website regularly for updates. For periods of poor visibility or severe weather, the schedule may be adjusted. Travel time is approximately 25 minutes. No charge for service!

No vehicles except bicycles are allowed on the ferries.

The exterior upper decks of the ferries on the New Jersey side tend to be crowded. Instead of pushing to get a good view, try going to a different deck. The main deck is spacious and a good area for taking nice photos.

(www.siferry.com)

Q1. When is the earliest departure time from Manhattan on Mondays?

    A. 12:00 a.m.

    B. 6:30 a.m.

    C. 12:00 p.m.

Q2. Which is true?

    A. Its schedule may be changed.

    B. The view on the New Jersey side isn't popular.

    C. Travel time is over half an hour.

Q3. Where is this information most likely found?

    A. On the company website

    B. At the train station

    C. At the hotel

Numbers 　　　　　　　　 CD 56

音声を聞き、書き取りなさい。

＜ Money（U.S.）＞

例： one dollar bill ($1), one penny (1¢), one nickel (5¢),
　　 one dime (10¢), one quarter (25¢)

(1) _____　(2) _____　(3) _____
(4) _____　(5) _____

異文化コミュニケーション
非言語コミュニケーション

　異文化において、言語が異なるということはわかりやすい違いだが、表情、視線、ジェスチャー等を含む非言語コミュニケーションの違いは見落とされやすい。例えば、日本では話し相手をじっと見つめることは往々にして礼儀に反するとされているが、視線を合わせないと誰に向かって話しているのかわからないと感じる文化もある。さらに、視線を合わせなければ話すことができない文化も存在する。また、文化が異なるとジェスチャーも異なる。例えば、日本では写真撮影の際に2本指を立ててピースサインを出す人が多い。しかし、指を立てることは侮蔑や悪態を表現することもあり、誤解の原因にもなりかねない。異なる文化の人と接触することは、日常の自分の動作や態度を異なる視点から捉える機会でもあり、コミュニケーションスキルを磨くきっかけにもなる。

Survival Activity
あなただったらどうする？
＜ケース 11＞
電車の駅で券売機の使い方がわからない。
このような場面に遭遇した時、あなたならどう対処するか考えてみよう。
また、その時に使える英語表現を考え、ロールプレイをしてみよう。

Unit 12　Renting a bike

Vocabulary

次の語句の意味を下から選びなさい。

1. sidewalk ( )		2. pathway ( )		
3. state ( )		4. agreement ( )		
5. clockwise ( )		6. inspect ( )		
7. retail ( )		8. vehicle ( )		
9. pedestrian ( )		10. equipment ( )		
11. obey ( )		12. define ( )		
13. yield ( )		14. replacement ( )		
15. voluntarily ( )				

歩道	時計回りの	州	小売り	車両
契約	歩行者	…を譲る	…を詳しく調べる	自由意思で
器具	取り替え	小道	…と定義する	…に従う

Comprehension Check 57

音声を聞き、正しい答えを選びなさい。

Scene 1 <At the bicycle rental shop ① >

(1) She wants to rent a bike for (half a day / a few hours).

(2) The rental price includes (insurance / locks).

Scene 2 <At the bicycle rental shop ② >

(1) You must obey (state / federal) laws when you ride a bike.

(2) There are bike lanes on the (streets / sidewalks).

Scene 3 <At the bicycle rental shop ③ >

(1) She (complains about / apologizes for) the incident.

(2) She will (pay for the damage / not get the refund).

Listening 58

音声を聞き、(　　　) を埋めなさい。

Central Park is a wonderful place for a relaxed riding experience. On a bike, you can see many locations in the park in a short amount of (①   ). One of the great advantages to biking in Central Park is that the main paths throughout the park are often closed to car traffic. In addition, cyclists may choose from three long-distance (②   ) of 6.1 miles, 5.2 miles or 1.7 miles. There are also some (③   ) routes crossing through the park at a number of locations. Cyclists are (④   ) to ride in a counterclockwise direction and it is (⑤   ) to ride on the pathways. Also, you must know that (⑥   ) always have the right of way.

Unit 12　Renting a bike

🔵 Pronunciation　　　🎧 59

次の自転車用語を英語で書き、音声を聞いて発音しなさい。

自転車	(	)	ペダル	(	)
ハンドル	(	)	ブレーキ	(	)
サドル	(	)	タイヤ	(	)
チェーン	(	)	車輪	(	)
ギア	(	)			

🔵 Useful Expressions　　　🎧 60

ペアで練習しなさい。

1. (A) Which do you like the best?
   (B) I like the red one.
2. (A) What do you think the prettiest season is?
   (B) I think spring is the prettiest.
3. (A) What is the most popular place?
   (B) The Empire State Building.
4. (A) Which is the least expensive gift?
   (B) Postcards are the least expensive.

🌐 Reading

次の文を読み、Q１～Q３に答えなさい。

Bike Park INC. rent-a-bike-centralpark.com

333.234.3692 40 West 55th Street. NY

NAME: _Mariya Suzuki_

ADDRESS/HOTEL: _New York Hotel_

OF PERSONS: ___2___

HOURS: (1) (②) (3) (Add.) _____

CHECK-IN: _1:00_ P.M. CHECK-OUT: _____

TOTAL AMOUNT PAID: ___$30_____

☑HELMET _2_ ☑BASKET _2_ ☑LOCKS _2_

RENTAL AGREEMENT

I accept for use, as it is, the equipment in good condition and accept full responsibility for care of the equipment while in my possession. I will be responsible for quick replacement at full retail value of all rental equipment if not returned or damaged, other than reasonable wear and tear, through the use of the equipment.

All instructions on the use of rental equipment have been made clear to me.

I have signed this agreement voluntarily and freely:

SIGNATURE: × _____Mariya Suzuki_____

Unit 12   Renting a bike

Q1. Where can this form most likely be found?

   A. At a police station

   B. At a restaurant

   C. At a rental shop

Q2. For how many hours is she going to rent it?

   A. Thirty minutes

   B. An hour and a half

   C. Two hours

Q3. What do people have to do in case of damage?

   A. Replace it quickly

   B. Report it to the police

   C. Claim insurance

🌐 Numbers 　　　　　　　💿 61

音声を聞き、書き取りなさい。

< Distances >

例： 1.55 miles

(1) _____　(2) _____　(3) _____
(4) _____　(5) _____

🧳 Travel Tips
交通ルール

　多くの国で車両は右側を通行する。しかし、古代ローマから中世までは左側通行が主流だった。旅をするということ自体が危険との出会いを意味した時代には危険に備えるため利き手の右手で武器を持ち、左手で馬車の手綱を引いていたことに由来する。いつから右側通行になったかについては諸説あるが、現在では大多数が右側通行である。一方、英国の影響をうけた国や地域（日本も含む）は左側通行である。沖縄では1972年に日本に返還される際に右側か左側かと議論になった。右側通行の国では、歩行者が横断歩道を渡る際にまず左を見る。海外旅行の際には交通ルールが日本とは異なることに十分留意し、事故に合わないよう、事故を起こさないよう気をつけよう。

Survival Activity
あなただったらどうする？
＜ケース12＞
道に迷って自転車を返す時刻に間に合いそうにない。

このような場面に遭遇した時、あなたならどう対処するか考えてみよう。
また、その時に使える英語表現を考え、ロールプレイをしてみよう。

Unit 13　Finding your way around

Vocabulary

次の語句の意味を下から選びなさい。

1. closure　　　（　　　　）　　2. bother　　　　（　　　　）
3. accommodate（　　　　）　　4. alternative　　（　　　　）
5. be aware　　（　　　　）　　6. encourage　　（　　　　）
7. contribute　（　　　　）　　8. complicated　（　　　　）
9. adjacent　　（　　　　）　　10. establishment（　　　　）
11. specifically（　　　　）　　12. subscriber　　（　　　　）
13. toll　　　　（　　　　）　　14. outskirts　　（　　　　）
15. annual　　（　　　　）

郊外	毎年の	加入者	使用料	具体的に
閉鎖	隣接した	…に寄付する	受け入れる	施設
代替の	…に手数をかける	複雑な	…に注意して	…を奨励する

Comprehension Check CD 62

音声を聞き、正しい答えを選びなさい。

Scene 1 <On the road ① >

(1) Penn Station is (a ten-minute walk from / next to) 7th Avenue.

(2) Penn Station is located on the (second / third) corner.

Scene 2 <On the road ② >

(1) The post office is (within walking distance / too far to walk).

(2) The post office is on the (left / right) side of the road.

Scene 3 <On the road ③ >

(1) After the traffic lights, make a (left / right) turn.

(2) The bookstore is located (opposite / adjacent) to the supermarket.

Listening CD 63

音声を聞き、(　　　) を埋めなさい。

Our office is located in Blue Park, on the outskirts of New York. The (①   ) way to get there from the airport is to take Interstate 20, which is a (②   ) road. Let me explain how the toll gate works. The toll gate is the (③   ) to the highway. It costs two dollars and twenty-five cents. At the gate, there are three types of (④   ): red, yellow and green. Red lanes are for drivers who don't have exact (⑤   ). Those who do have exact change use the yellow lanes. The green lanes are for (⑥   ) subscribers, who have a radio-magnetic device in their cars.

Unit 13　Finding your way around

🌐 Pronunciation　　🎧 64

次の語句を英語で書き、音声を聞いて発音しなさい。

ポスト	(	)	ロータリー	(	)
ガソリンスタンド	(	)	駐車場	(	)
ジョギングコース	(	)	銀行	(	)
シンボルマーク	(	)	図書館	(	)
交差点	(	)			

🌐 Useful Expressions　　🎧 65

ペアで練習しなさい。

1. (A) Is there a grocery store in front of the church?
   (B) No, but there's one behind it.

2. (A) Is the bank next to the supermarket?
   (B) No, it's opposite to the supermarket.

3. (A) Is the movie theater past the traffic light?
   (B) No, it's just before the traffic light.

4. (A) Is there a public restroom near here?
   (B) Yes, follow the street by the park. You can't miss it.

Reading

次の掲示を読み、Q1～Q3に答えなさい。

**BE AWARE
PLAN AHEAD
SATURDAY MAR. 25**

**ROAD CLOSURE
NOTICE**

EVENT INFORMATION

THE CITY MARATHON & 1/2 MARATHON

will start at 7:00 a.m. from the park entrance.
Please be advised that the annual City Marathon will run through your neighborhood on Saturday March 25. This charity event has contributed over $1 million for many local establishments. Join us on the route to support more than 15,000 participants from over 50 countries.

Roads around Central Park are subject to closure to traffic from approximately 5:00 a.m. to 9:00 a.m. to accommodate runners.
Detailed road closure information is available by contacting 1-800-000-1188.
Detailed race route maps are available on the race web page.

www.citymarathonny.com

Q1. What is the purpose of the notice?

　　A. To recruit more participants

　　B. To support runners

　　C. To encourage taking an alternative route

Q2. Which statement is NOT true?

　　A. The runners have to be local residents.

　　B. Two different distances are possible in this event.

　　C. This marathon is held once a year.

Q3. How can people get further information about the closure?

　　A. Visiting the website

　　B. Dropping in at the management office

　　C. Calling the number

Numbers 🎧 66

音声を聞き、書き取りなさい。

< Four or More Digits >

例： 10,000

(1) _____　(2) _____　(3) _____
(4) _____　(5) _____

異文化コミュニケーション
対人距離

　多くの人はひとりで電車に乗る時、端の席、あるいは隣が空いている席に座る。他に空いている席がたくさんあるのにもかかわらず、知らない人が自分の横に座ると快適さが損なわれるのは縄張り意識が働くからだと考えられている。縄張りの距離は文化や民族、年齢、男女、相手との関係によって異なる。日本では満員電車や、定員いっぱいになるまでエレベーターに乗るなど、見知らぬ他人との身体接触が頻繁に起きるが、米国では他人との距離が日本人より広い。列を作って並ばなければならないような場合でも前後に広い間隔をあける。少しでもからだや荷物が人に接触しそうな、または接触した際には sorry、あるいは excuse me 等の軽い謝罪表現を使う。

Survival Activity
あなただったらどうする？

＜ケース 13 ＞

滞在先のホテルに戻る途中に道に迷った。

このような場面に遭遇した時、あなたならどう対処するか考えてみよう。
また、その時に使える英語表現を考え、ロールプレイをしてみよう。

Unit 14　Medical care

Vocabulary

次の語句の意味を下から選びなさい。

1. irritated　　　(　　　)　　2. pharmacist　　(　　　)
3. practical　　　(　　　)　　4. hurt　　　　　(　　　)
5. comprehensive (　　　)　　6. twist　　　　　(　　　)
7. prescription　(　　　)　　8. swell　　　　　(　　　)
9. associate　　 (　　　)　　10. rub　　　　　　(　　　)
11. ingest　　　 (　　　)　　12. over-the-counter (　　　)
13. minor　　　　(　　　)　　14. symptoms　　　(　　　)
15. physician　　(　　　)

痛む	…を関連させる	不快感がある	…をねじる	包括的な
薬剤師	…をこする	処方箋	…を摂取する	実用的な
症状	深刻でない	はれる	内科医	処方箋不要の

Comprehension Check 　CD 67

音声を聞き、正しい答えを選びなさい。

Scene 1 <At the pharmacy>

(1) Her eyes are (irritated / sore).

(2) The tablets are to be taken every (two / four) hours.

Scene 2 <At the hotel>

(1) She might have eaten something (bad / spicy) at lunch.

(2) She will (wait for a doctor / go see a doctor).

Scene 3 <At the doctor's office>

(1) She twisted her ankle a couple of (hours / days) ago.

(2) She (has gotten / will get) medicine.

Listening 　CD 68

音声を聞き、(　　　) を埋めなさい。

In my previous travels abroad, I had never considered the (①　　　　) for travel insurance. All that (②　　　　) when, in the small mountains of Australia, I was thrown from a (③　　　　). The left side of my leg and shoulder were seriously injured. It would have taken more than two hours to reach the nearest (④　　　　) in the worst-case (⑤　　　　). Fortunately, XYZ Worldwide Insurance's comprehensive plan got me to medical care with an interpreter. Exploring the world makes a beautiful experience and (⑥　　　　) travel insurance is just a practical necessity of travel.

Unit 14　Medical care

🌐 Pronunciation　　🎧 69

次の語句を英語で書き、音声を聞いて発音しなさい。

ビタミン	(	)	アレルギー	(	)
熱	(	)	バンドエイド	(	)
ガーゼ	(	)	ウィルス	(	)
エネルギー	(	)	腹痛	(	)
頭痛	(	)			

🌐 Useful Expressions　　🎧 70

ペアで練習しなさい。

1. (A) I have a sunburn.
   (B) You should apply some after-sun cream.
2. (A) My eyes are itchy.
   (B) Then you probably shouldn't rub your eyes.
3. (A) I'm getting motion sickness.
   (B) Try not to think about it.
4. (A) I want to take my temperature.
   (B) You can use this thermometer.

『The Rod and Serpent of Asklepios』蛇杖のシンボルは、医術・医学の象徴として世界的に広く用いられ、WHO（世界保健機構）の切手のデザインとして、また多くの国々で救急医療を表すロゴとしても採用されています。

Reading

次の文を読みQ1～Q3に答えなさい。

Over-the-counter cold/flu relief

Uses: For temporary relief of the following minor symptoms when associated with the common cold or flu: fever, aches and pains including headache and muscular aches associated with fever, runny nose and sneezing, nasal congestion, cough and/or pain due to bronchial irritation.

Directions: For adults and children 12 years or older. Take 2 tablespoons orally. Wait 6 hours, and repeat dosage if symptoms return. Do not exceed 4 doses in a 24-hour period.

Stop using and ask a doctor if
- pain, cough, or nasal congestion gets worse or lasts more than 7 days
- new symptoms occur
- dizziness or sleeplessness occur
- fever gets worse or lasts more than 3 days

<u>Notes</u>
nasal congestion　鼻詰まり
bronchial irritation　気管支の炎症
dizziness　めまい

Q1. What is this product used for?

   A. To protect a medicine taker from the cold/flu

   B. To relieve any symptoms of sickness

   C. To relieve typical symptoms of the cold

Q2. How should you use this product?

   A. Ingest through your mouth

   B. Apply evenly all over your body

   C. Take after dissolving in water

Q3. How can people get this product?

   A. See a physician

   B. Go to a drug store

   C. Get a prescription

🔵 Numbers 　　　　　　　　🎧 71

音声を聞き、書き取りなさい。

< Frequencies >

例： once an hour, every five minutes

(1) _____　(2) _____　(3) _____
(4) _____　(5) _____

🧳 Travel Tips
具合が悪くなった時

　薬が簡単に入手できなかった時代には、その土地の風土習慣を生かした様々な智恵が利用されてきた。例えば、日本では腹痛を起こしたら梅干しを食べると良い、という言い伝えがある。ヨーロッパではお腹の調子が悪い時は、消化を助けてリラックスさせる効果があるというカモミールティーを飲むのが一般的だ。そのような習慣は古代エジプト、ギリシャ、ローマ時代からあるという。地中海地方ではオリーブオイルを一匙飲む。オリーブオイルは「地中海式ダイエット（食事療法）」の代表的食材でもあり、健康に良いと注目されている。エジプトでは5000年前からモロヘイヤを栽培しており、風邪をひいた時、モロヘイヤスープを飲む。英国では、紅茶を1日に何度も飲むが、2006年にストレスホルモンに良い影響を与える物質を含んでいることが科学的に証明された*。

* UCL (University College of London) の研究者によって2006年 *The Journal of Psychopharmacology* で発表された。

Survival Activity
あなただったらどうする？
＜ケース 14 ＞
持病の花粉症の症状が出て、薬局で自分の症状を説明して薬を買いたい。

　このような場面に遭遇した時、あなたならどう対処するか考えてみよう。
また、その時に使える英語表現を考え、ロールプレイをしてみよう。

Unit 15　Leaving for home

Vocabulary

次の語句の意味を下から選びなさい。

1. questionnaire （　　　　　）　　2. acceptance （　　　　　）
3. extreme （　　　　　）　　4. labor （　　　　　）
5. opportunity （　　　　　）　　6. appreciate （　　　　　）
7. diverse （　　　　　）　　8 dated （　　　　　）
9. curb （　　　　　）　　10. tolerance （　　　　　）
11. survive （　　　　　）　　12. comfort （　　　　　）
13. rate （　　　　　）　　14. prompt （　　　　　）
15. renovate （　　　　　）

極端な	機会	多様な	労働（者）	…を認識する
素早い	アンケート	時代遅れの	…を修復する	快適さ
寛容	受容すること	…を評価付けする	縁石	生き残る

Comprehension Check CD 72

音声を聞き、正しい答えを選びなさい。

Scene 1 <At the hotel>

(1) She will fill out the form (before / after) she leaves the hotel.

(2) She is going to take (a taxi / a bus).

Scene 2 <In the taxi>

(1) She pays ($55.00 / $80.00)

(2) Passengers can get off on (only one side / either side) of the taxi.

Scene 3 <At the airport>

(1) The flight will be delayed for (two / three) hours.

(2) The new flight arrives in Tokyo at (14:10 / 15:55).

Listening CD 73

音声を聞き、(　　　) を埋めなさい。

Postcards from California are always (①   ). But when you get there, it rains. When you want to fly, flights are canceled or delayed because of extreme weather. The hotel may be (②   ). The museum might be closed due to labor strikes. You may run into various troubles while you travel. But you can survive. Traveling can be a fun (③   ). Travels can be a great (④   ) tool. There are many places in the world you can go. You can educate yourself by opening yourself to the world. Time spent (⑤   ) helps you understand and appreciate diverse (⑥   ). In addition, it encourages acceptance and tolerance of ways of life that differ from your own. It makes you a better person.

Unit 15 Leaving for home

🌀 Pronunciation 💿 74

次の国名・都市名を英語で書き、音声を聞いて発音しなさい。

韓国	(	)	タイ王国	(	)
フィリピン	(	)	ベトナム	(	)
インドネシア	(	)	インド	(	)
ブラジル	(	)	アルゼンチン	(	)
北京	(	)			

🌀 Useful Expressions 💿 75

ペアで練習しなさい。

1. (A) Make it thirty dollars.

    (B) Thank you. Twenty dollars is your change.

2. (A) Keep the change.

    (B) Thank you. Would you like a receipt?

3. (A) Can you give me change for a hundred dollar bill?

    (B) Sorry, I can't break that.

4. (A) Do you have change for a fifty dollar bill?

    (B) Do you have any smaller bills?

Reading

次の表を読み、Q1～Q3に答えなさい。

Please take a moment to rate our service.
Thank you for giving us an opportunity to serve you.

	5. Super	4. Excellent	3. Good	2. Fair	1. Poor
Overall experience	5.	**(4.)**	3.	2.	1.
Check-in					
Service	**(5.)**	4.	3.	2.	1.
Speed	**(5.)**	4.	3.	2.	1.
Room					
Value	5.	**(4.)**	3.	2.	1.
Comfort	5.	4.	**(3.)**	2	1.
Cleanliness	5.	**(4.)**	3.	2.	1.
Food and Restaurant if used					
Variety	5.	4.	3.	2.	1.
Quality of food and drinks	5.	4.	3.	2.	1.
Hotel staff					
Friendliness	**(5.)**	4.	3.	2.	1.
Prompt service	**(5.)**	4.	3.	2.	1.
Check-out					
Convenience	**(5.)**	4.	3.	2.	1.

Additional comment: *Although the room was a little dated, it was clean and comfortable. The location is fairly good and central, with easy access to many attractions.*

Unit 15 Leaving for home

Q1. Who conducted the survey?

   A. A hotel

   B. A restaurant

   C. A travel agency

Q2. What is suggested by this form?

   A. The customer was not satisfied with the check-in procedure.

   B. The customer was not satisfied with the staff.

   C. The customer didn't eat in the establishment.

Q3. What is mentioned about the facility?

   A. The facility is not in walking distance from attractions.

   B. The facility is small but comfortable.

   C. The facility hasn't been renovated recently.

Numbers   76
音声を聞き、書き取りなさい。

< Times 2 >

   例：12:15

(1) _____   (2) _____   (3) _____

(4) _____   (5) _____

Travel Tips
航空便の遅延

　日常生活に比べて行動半径が広くなる旅行にはさまざまなトラブルが起きる可能性がある。例えば、交通機関の遅延や運航中止等を考慮して余裕のあるスケジュールを組むことが必要である。航空機遅延の補償程度や内容は、航空会社や航空券の種類、代金などによって異なる。そのため購入時にしっかりと把握しておくことが大切だ。航空会社に責任が問えるのは、航空会社のストや機体整備に起因する遅延や欠航等である。戦争やテロ、天候などの不可抗力による遅延や運航中止の際に生じる費用、宿泊費等は航空会社の免責事項である。しかし、それらの費用をまかなう保険を海外旅行保険に付帯し、万が一に備えることもできる。

Survival Activity

あなただったらどうする？
＜ケース 15 ＞
滞在先のホテルのサービスがとても良かったのでスタッフに直接お礼を言いたい。

　このような場面に遭遇した時、あなたならどう対処するか考えてみよう。
　また、その時に使える英語表現を考え、ロールプレイをしてみよう。

Additional Activities

Pair Work with Numbers

ここでは、本文の各 Unit に掲載されている Numbers の復習として、数字などの読み方をペアで練習する。

【手順】
1. 2人組になり Student A と Student B を決める。
2. Student A は Student A と表記されている左側の偶数ページの指示に従いなさい。
   Student B は Student B と表記されている右側の奇数ページの指示に従いなさい。
3. お互いに答え合わせをしなさい。

Student A (Student B は P. 99 へ)

Student A

Unit 1【Flight Numbers】A

1. 次の航空機便名を読み上げなさい。

   例：NH1122（N-H-one-one-two-two）

   NH3564   AA4571   UA1783   NZ8015   DL1179

2. Student B が読み上げる航空機便名を聞いて書き取りなさい。

   _____

Unit 2【Seat Numbers】A

1. 次の飛行機の座席番号を読み上げなさい。

   例：10A（ten-A）

   30D   40H   51J   13A   57C

2. Student B が読み上げる座席番号を聞いて書き取りなさい。

   _____

Unit 3【Durations of Time】A

1. 次の時間を読み上げなさい。

   例：2 hours (two hours), 45 minutes (forty-five minutes), 30 seconds (thirty seconds)

   3 hours   20 minutes   10 seconds   15 minutes   two and a half hours

2. Student B が読み上げる時間を聞いて書き取りなさい。

   _____

Pair Work with Numbers

ここでは、本文の各 Unit に掲載されている Numbers の復習として、数字などの読み方をペアで練習する。

【手順】
1. 2人組になり Student A と Student B を決める。
2. Student A は Student A と表記されている左側の偶数ページの指示に従いなさい。
   Student B は Student B と表記されている右側の奇数ページの指示に従いなさい。
3. お互いに答え合わせをしなさい。

⬅ Student A は P. 98 へ　**Student B**

Student B

Unit 1【Flight Numbers】B

1. 次の航空機便名を読み上げなさい。

   例：NH1122（N-H-one-one-two-two）

   JL001　CX1234　SQ9876　BA0012　KL4234

2. Student A が読み上げる航空機便名を聞いて書き取りなさい。

Unit 2【Seat Numbers】B

1. 次の飛行機の座席番号を読み上げなさい。

   例：10A（ten-A）

   41E　30F　12C　25A　57D

2. Student A が読み上げる座席番号を聞いて書き取りなさい。

Unit 3【Durations of Time】B

1. 次の時間を読み上げなさい。

   例：2 hours (two hours), 45 minutes (forty-five minutes), 30 seconds (thirty seconds)

   4 hours　10 minutes　30 seconds　25 minutes　three and a half hours

2. Student A が読み上げる時間を聞いて書き取りなさい。

Student A Student B は P. 101 へ

Unit 4【Dates】A

1. 次の日付を読み上げなさい。

   例：5/26/2001 (May twenty-sixth, two thousand and one/twenty oh one)

   11/1/1998   8/1/2020   1/10/2005   2/14/1968   6/24/2015

2. Student B が読み上げる日付を聞いて書き取りなさい。

   _____

Unit 5【Times 1】A

1. 次の時刻を読み上げなさい。

   例：5:00 (Five o'clock), 5:30 (five thirty/half past five/half after five)

   7:00   11:00   12:30   5:30   12:00

2. Student B が読み上げる時刻を聞いて書き取りなさい。

   _____

Unit 6【Fractions】A

1. 次の分数を読み上げなさい。

   例：1/3 (one third), 2/3 (two thirds)

   1/10   1/2   3/4   5/6   1/20

2. Student B が読み上げる分数を聞いて書き取りなさい。

   _____

Unit 7【Prices 1】A

1. 次の価格を読み上げなさい。

   例：$110 (one hundred (and) ten dollars/a hundred (and) ten dollars)

   $18 $80 $150 $290 $460

2. Student B が読み上げる価格を聞いて書き取りなさい。

   _____

Student A は P.100 へ | **Student B**

Unit 4 【Dates】B

1. 次の日付を読み上げなさい。

    例：5/26/2001（May twenty-sixth, two thousand and one/twenty oh one）

    10/5/1997   3/26/2016   4/30/2007   7/17/1996   9/20/2016

2. Student A が読み上げる日付を聞いて書き取りなさい。

    _____

Unit 5 【Times 1】B

1. 次の時刻を読み上げなさい。

    例：5:00 (Five o'clock) 5:30 (five thirty/half past five/half after five)

    6:00   10:00   2:30   4:30   12:00

2. Student A が読み上げる時刻を聞いて書き取りなさい。

    _____

Unit 6 【Fractions】B

1. 次の分数を読み上げなさい。

    例：1/3 (one third), 2/3 (two thirds)

    1/20   1/4   3/5   3/10   1/100

2. Student A が読み上げる分数を聞いて書き取りなさい。

    _____

Unit 7 【Prices 1】B

1. 次の価格を読み上げなさい。

    例：$110 (one hundred (and) ten dollars/a hundred (and) ten dollars)

    $19 $70 $145 $299 $830

2. Student A が読み上げる価格を聞いて書き取りなさい。

    _____

Student A　Student B は P. 103 へ

Unit 8 【Prices 2】 A

1. 次の価格を読み上げなさい。

例：$50.25 (fifty dollars and twenty-five cents/fifty twenty-five)

$10.10　$12.25　$70.75　$119.99　$230.50

2. Student B が読み上げる価格を聞いて書き取りなさい。

Unit 9 【Phone Numbers】 A

1. 次の電話番号を読み上げなさい。

例：555-2079 (five five five two oh seven nine)

212-6789　505-2143　920-2000　351-1207　313-4068

2. Student B が読み上げる電話番号を聞いて書き取りなさい。

Unit 10 【Street Names】 A

1. 次の通りの名前を読み上げなさい。

例：2nd Street (Second Street)

4th Street　21st Street　17th Street　32nd Street　23rd Street

2. Student B が読み上げる通りの名前を聞いて書き取りなさい。

Unit 11 【Money (U.S.)】 A

1. 次の金額を通称で読み上げなさい。

例：one dollar (bill)/a dollar (bill) ($1), one penny (1¢), one nickel (5¢), one dime (10¢), one quarter (25¢)

two dollars　two pennies　four nickels　three dimes　three quarters

2. Student B が読み上げる金額を聞いて書き取りなさい。

Student B

Student A は P. 102 へ

Unit 8 【Prices 2】 B

1. 次の価格を読み上げなさい。

   例：$50.25 (fifty dollars and twenty-five cents/fifty twenty-five))

   $20.10 $12.05 $60.75 $190.99 $372.50

2. Student A が読み上げる価格を聞いて書き取りなさい。

___

Unit 9 【Phone Numbers】 B

1. 次の電話番号を読み上げなさい。

   例：555-2079 (five five five two oh seven nine)

   315-9876   202-3142   890-5696   751-2607   402-5612

2. Student A が読み上げる電話番号を聞いて書き取りなさい。

___

Unit 10 【Street Names】 B

1. 次の通りの名前を読み上げなさい。

   例：2nd Street（Second Street）

   5th Street   31st Street   14th Street   22nd Street   17th Street

2. Student A が読み上げる通りの名前を聞いて書き取りなさい。

___

Unit 11 【Money (U.S.)】 B

1. 次の金額を通称で読み上げなさい。

   例：one dollar (bill)/a dollar (bill) ($1), one penny (1¢), one nickel (5¢), one dime (10¢), one quarter (25¢)

   five dollars   ten pennies   six nickels   two dimes   three quarters

2. Student A が読み上げる金額を聞いて書き取りなさい。

Student A Student B は P. 105 へ

Unit 12 【Distances】 A

1. 次の距離を読み上げなさい。

    例： 1.55 miles (one point five five miles)

    1.2 miles   5.01 miles   9.53 miles   0.13 miles   2.56 miles

2. Student B が読み上げる距離を聞いて書き取りなさい。

    _____

Unit 13 【Four or More Digits】 A

1. 次の 4 桁以上の数字を読み上げなさい。

    例： 10,000 (ten thousand)

    30,000   12,500   2,678,299   123,456,789,000   100,000,000,000

2. Student B が読み上げる 4 桁以上の数字を聞いて書き取りなさい。

    _____

Unit 14 【Frequencies】 A

1. 次の頻度を表す表現を読み上げなさい。

    例： once an hour, every five minutes

    twice every three hours   four times a day   five days a week
    every ten minutes   once a week

2. Student B が読み上げる頻度を表す表現を聞いて書き取りなさい。

    _____

Unit 15 【Times 2】 A

1. 次の時刻を読み上げなさい。

    例： 12:15 (twelve fifteen/a quarter past twelve/a quarter after twelve)

    2:10   4:50   5:55   11:45   3:05

2. Student B が読み上げる時刻を聞いて書き取りなさい。

    _____

Student A は P. 104 へ　**Student B**

Unit 12【Distances】B

1. 次の距離を読み上げなさい。

   例：1.55 miles (one point five five miles)

   1.9 miles　6.01 miles　8.56 miles　0.43 miles　3.52 miles

2. Student A が読み上げる距離を聞いて書き取りなさい。

Unit 13【Four or More Digits】B

1. 次の4桁以上の数字を読み上げなさい。

   例：10,000 (ten thousand)

   20,000　13,500　2,456,399　987,654,321,000　300,000,000,000

2. Student A が読み上げる4桁以上の数字を聞いて書き取りなさい。

Unit 14【Frequencies】B

1. 次の頻度を表す表現を読み上げなさい。

   例：once an hour, every five minutes

   twice every five hours　six times a day　four days a month
   every twenty minutes　two days a week

2. Student A が読み上げる頻度を表す表現を聞いて書き取りなさい。

Unit 15【Times 2】B

1. 次の時刻を読み上げなさい。

   例：12:15 (twelve fifteen/a quarter past twelve/a quarter after twelve)

   3:10　9:50　2:55　7:45　8:05

2. Student A が読み上げる時刻を聞いて書き取りなさい。

Script for Comprehension Check

Unit 1

Comprehension Check

Scene 1 <At the check-in counter>

(C: Check-in clerk   T: Tourist)

C: May I see your passport, please?

T: Sure.

C: Have you already checked in on the web?

T: Yes, but I haven't printed my boarding pass yet.

C: All right. Will you be checking a piece of baggage?

T: Yes.

C: All right. Could you put your bag on the scale? Thank you. Ah, the suitcase weighs 24 kilograms, which is a little over our allowance. Would you like to pay the extra fee?

T: Oh! How much do I have to pay?

C: We must charge you an extra….

T: Ah, I know! I can carry my electric gadgets with me in the carry-on bag. I think they're more than two kilograms.

Scene 2 <At the security checkpoint>

(S: Security officer   T: Tourist)

S: May I see your boarding pass?

T: Sure.

S: Okay. Please place all metal items in the tray and take your laptop out of its case.

T: What about liquids? Do I have to take them out, too?

S: Yes, ma'am. Also, remove your coat and empty your pockets before proceeding through the body scanner.

T: Okay.

Scene 3 <At the information counter>

(I: Information counter clerk   T: Tourist)

T: They just made the gate change announcement, but I couldn't really catch it. Could you tell me the new one?

I: Sure, may I have your flight number and departure time?

T: It's AB 123 to JFK and the departure time is 6:50.

I: Let me see. Okay, the departure gate has changed from D56 to E80. You must go there now.

T: Where is it?

I: Take the shuttle train from downstairs. It takes you to the E gate area.

T: Thank you.

Unit 2   7

Comprehension Check

Scene 1 < On the plane ① >

(C: Cabin attendant   T: Tourist)

    C: Hi, welcome on board. What's your seat number?

    T: 35C.

    C: That's on the right side of the aisle.

    T: I see, thank you.

        (After a while)

    T: Excuse me, I think you're in my seat.

Man: Oh, let me check my boarding pass. Oh, you're right. I'm sorry.

Scene 2 <On the plane ② >

(C: Cabin attendant   T: Tourist)

    T: Excuse me.

    C: Yes, how can I help you?

    T: My headset doesn't seem to be working properly.

    C: Oh, let me see. You're right. I'll bring another set. Just a moment.

    T: Thank you. Can I also have a blanket? I'm a little cold.

    C: Sure, I'll be right back.

Scene 3 <On the plane ③ >

(C: Cabin attendant   T: Tourist)

    C: Is beef all right for your lunch?

    T: Can I have fish?

    C: I'm sorry, but we're all out of fish. But we do have a vegetarian menu. It's pasta with broccoli. Would you prefer that?

    T: Yes, please.

    C: Here you go. What would you like to drink with your meal?

    T: A coke, please.

Unit 3 🎧 12

Comprehension Check

Scene 1 <At the immigration booth>

(I: Immigration officer   T: Tourist)

    I: Your passport and customs form please.

    T: Here you are.

    I: How long are you staying?

    T: About one week.

    I: What's the purpose of your stay?

    T: Sightseeing.

    I: Fine. Place your four left fingers on the scanner.

    T: Sorry? I didn't understand what you said.

    I: First, put your four left fingers here on this device. We're taking your fingerprints. Now your thumb, please.

    T: Was that okay?

    I: Good, now for your right hand. Good. Now look at the camera. We're taking your photo now.

Scene 2 <At the lost-and-found office>

(G: Ground staff   T: Tourist)

    T: Excuse me, but my bag didn't come out of the baggage carousel.

    G: May I see your ticket and claims tag?

    T: Sure.

    G: You checked in your baggage at Haneda Airport, correct?

    T: Yes, I did.

    G: Please describe your bag. What does it look like?

    T: Well, it's a hard-shell type suitcase.

    G: What color is it?

    T: It's red with a polka-dot belt.

    G: With a belt… all right. Where are you staying in the US?

    T: I'm staying at New York Hotel in Manhattan. This is the address.

    G: All right. We will send your bag to the hotel when it arrives. Here is your Delayed Baggage Report.

    T: Very well. Thank you.

Scene 3 <Ground transportation>

(I: Information clerk   T: Tourist)

    T: Hi, I have a booking for a share taxi service to Manhattan and I was supposed to meet a clerk at the counter, but nobody seems to be there.

    I: It's probably a little too early. You can use the phone on the wall to call courtesy if you want. Somebody in the office will help you.

    T: Do I need coins to call?

    I: No, you don't. It's free of charge.

Unit 4 🎧 17

Comprehension Check

Scene 1   <At the front desk ① >

(F: Front clerk   T: Tourist)

    T: Hi, I have a reservation under Suzuki for one for six nights.

    F: Welcome to New York Hotel. May I see your ID, please?

    T: Sure, here you are.

    F: Thank you. Hmm… I'm sorry but I can't find your reservation. How did you make your reservation? Did you make one directly with us, or did you use a travel agent?

    T: I reserved the room through an on-line hotel reservation service. I have a confirmation sheet.

    F: Thank you. Yes, I see. There might be a mistake with the booking system. I apologize. Okay, we do have a room for you.

Scene 2   <At the front desk ② >

(F: Front clerk   T: Tourist)

    F: We offer a complimentary continental breakfast served from 6:00 a.m. to 10:00 a.m. on weekdays and to 10:30 a.m. on weekends.

    T: That sounds nice. Where is it served?

    F: In the lounge. It's right on the left, at that corner over there.

    T: Do I need to show a voucher or something for the breakfast?

    F: No, you don't. You just go in and tell them your room number.

    T: I see. Thank you.

Scene 3   <At the front desk ③ >

(F: Front clerk   T: Tourist)

    T: Excuse me. I'm having a problem with my room key.

    F: What's wrong?

    T: It doesn't work. I can't even open the door.

    F: The black side of the card goes into the slot. Then you swipe it slowly.

    T: I know, but it doesn't work.

    F: Oh, I apologize for the inconvenience. I'll re-program the card for you right away.

Unit 5 💿 22

Comprehension Check

Scene 1 <At the front desk>

(F: Front clerk   T: Tourist)

    T: Hi. We'd like to do some sightseeing. What would you suggest?

    F: Well, what kind of things would you like to see?

    T: Whatever is fine. This is my first visit to New York.

    F: Okay, then. I'd suggest taking a double-decker tour. They take you to most of the major sights. It's nice for first time visitors and not too expensive.

    T: How much does it cost?

    F: Seventy-five dollars per person for two days.

    T: Really? That doesn't sound too expensive. We might do that. Can I have a brochure?

Scene 2 <At the concierge desk ① >

(C: Concierge   T: Tourist)

[pointing to the brochure]

    T: How can I get to this place? Do I need a taxi?

    C: No, ma'am. You can walk. It's not far. It's only about a fifteen-minute walk.

    T: Okay, but could you tell me how to get there?

    C: Okay, here's a map of the city. We're here, turn right at the main entrance outside the hotel, and walk down 8th Street until here. It's about three blocks down. There's a big sign after this cathedral. You can't miss it.

Scene 3 <At the concierge desk ② >

(C: Concierge   T: Tourist)

    T: Do you know what the weather is going to be like today?

    C: Yes, the forecast says it'll be sunny during the day and around seventy degrees but in the evening it'll be cloudy with heavy showers.

    T: The evening doesn't sound too pleasant.

    C: Yeah, really. You'd better bring your umbrella.

    T: Ah, do you have an umbrella I could borrow?

    C: Sure. It's the last one. Could I just have you write your name and room number on the list?

Unit 6 💿 27

Comprehension Check

Scene 1 <At the sandwich shop>

(S: Shop clerk   T: Tourist)

    S: Hi, may I take your order?

    T: Hi, I'd like a mushroom and cucumber sandwich and a regular-size lemonade, please.

    S: Sure. Would you like white or brown bread?

    T: Brown, please.

    S: For here or to go?

    T: For here, please.

    S: That will be twelve twenty-five with tax.

    T: Here's a twenty.

    S: Seven dollars and seventy-five cents is your change. Have a nice day.

    T: You too.

Scene 2 <At the fast food restaurant>

(S: Shop clerk   T: Tourist)

    S: Hi, what would you like?

    T: May I have a pretzel and a mixed berry frozen yogurt, please?

    S: Which pretzel would you like? We have original, cinnamon and sugar.

    T: Let me see… I'll have an original. I don't like cinnamon.

    S: Anything else?

    T: That's it.

    S: That's twelve fifty.

    T: Pardon me? Twelve fifty?

    S: Er, let me check. Oh, I'm sorry. You chose an original, didn't you?

    T: Yes, I did.

    S: Okay. That comes to eleven fifty.

Scene 3 <At the burger shop>

(S: Shop clerk   T: Tourist)

    T: May I have a single hamburger, with a small crispy French fries?

    S: What would you like on your burger?

    T: Lettuce and mustard please.

    S: Would you like our original sauce on it as well? It's very nice.

    T: Okay, I'll try it.

    S: Please go to the counter to the right when your number is called.

[later]

    S: Number fifteen!

    T: I'm fifteen. Oh no. I ordered lettuce on my burger, not tomato.

    S: Oh, you did? I'll fix it right away. Sorry about that.

Unit 7 CD 32

Comprehension Check

Scene 1 <At the tourist information counter>

(C: Clerk T: Tourist)

    T: What's the most popular musical playing now?

    C: Well, we have long-running musicals such as *Phantom of the Opera, Chicago* and *the Lion King.*

    T: Do you think there are any tickets available for today?

    C: Probably. Why don't you go to the TKTS booth at Times Square? They sell same-day discount tickets for both matinée and evening performances.

    T: That may be a good idea, but you have to wait for over an hour, don't you?

    C: Yes, sometimes two or three hours.

Scene 2 <At the box office>

(C: Clerk T: Tourist)

    T: Do you have two tickets left for tonight?

    C: Yes. We have various prices from 26 to 122 dollars.

    T: Our budget is about seventy dollars.

    C: All right. What about seats in the rear orchestra? We have U six and U eight.

    T: Oh, would there be someone between us?

    C: No, you'd be together. Please look at our seat chart here. We have odd-number seats on the left of the theater and even-number seats on the right.

    T: I see. They seem like good seats. We'll take them.

Scene 3 <With the usher>

(U: Usher T: Tourist)

    T: Excuse me, could you take me to this seat?

    U: Certainly, please follow me. Here is your program.

    T: How long does the musical last?

    U: Two hours and thirty minutes.

    T: Is there an intermission?

    U: Yes. There's a twenty-minute intermission. You can go to the bar for beverages during that time.

Unit 8 🎧 37

Comprehension Check

Scene 1 <At the entrance>

(R: Receptionist T: Tourist)

T: We don't have a reservation, but we'd like a table for two by the window if possible.

R: No reservation? I don't think it'll be a problem. One second while I check if a table by the window is available.

T: Thanks.

(After a while)

R: Okay, we have a window side table for you. This way please.

(After being seated)

Your server will be right with you.

Scene 2 <Ordering food>

(S: Server T: Tourist)

S: Hi, how are you doing tonight? My name is Dennis, your server this evening.
Here are your menus. Can I get you folks a drink first?

T: Yes, I'll have a soda with lime, and my friend will have a glass of tap water without ice.

S: Sure. Would you like to start off your dinner with some appetizers?

T: Well, we are going to see a musical tonight. Could you tell me which dish can be served right away?

S: We are always ready for pre-theater diners, so don't worry about it.

T: Good, then we'll have appetizers and an entrée.

Scene 3 <Paying>

(S: Server T: Tourist)

S: Here's your check. Will you be paying with cash or credit?

T: We'd like to pay in cash. Is the tip included in the check?

S: Yes. Tax and gratuity have already been included.

T: Hold on. I'm afraid we ordered one glass of lemonade, not two.

S: Oh. Let me see. Yes, you're right. You ordered one glass. I'll get this corrected and be right back.

Unit 9

Comprehension Check

Scene 1 <At the shop>

(S: Sales person T: Tourist)

    S: Hi, how are you doing?

    T: I'm looking for a coat for myself.

    S: Ah, I see. Let me show you what we have right now. What size do you wear?

    T: I'm not quite sure about US sizes but I think Japanese size nine is equivalent to American two to four.

    S: Okay, this is size two and is a great deal. It was sixty-nine dollars, but today it's on sale for only thirty-nine.

    T: Perfect. May I try it on?

    S: Sure. The fitting room is right over there.

Scene 2 <With the cashier>

(C: Cashier T: Tourist)

    C: How will you be paying? Cash or charge?

    T: Charge, please.

    C: Could you just swipe your credit card through the terminal?

    T: Huh? It doesn't seem to work.

    C: May I see your card? I'm sorry, but the expiration date on this credit card has already passed.

    T: Oh, no! I didn't notice. Okay, let me use another one.

Scene 3 <At customer service>

(C: Clerk T: Tourist)

    T: Hi. I bought this sweater a couple hours ago but it's too large. Is it possible to exchange it for a smaller size?

    C: We have smaller sizes, but I don't think we have any more in black. You could exchange it for another color though.

    T: Oh, I really wanted to have it in black. Can I get a refund?

    C: If you have the receipt, sure.

Unit 10 🔘 47

Comprehension Check

Scene 1 <On the phone>

(T: Tourist   Taxi: Taxi Campany)

Taxi: Hello. Yellow Taxi.

T: Hello, I left a pair of glasses in the taxi this morning.

Taxi: Well, our drivers find lots of glasses every day. Can you describe them?

T: Yes. They are regular glasses with a black frame and are in a red plastic case. I can't see anything without them.

Taxi: Sorry, they don't seem to be here.

Scene 2 <With the security officer ① >

(S: Security officer   T: Tourist)

T: I've lost my purse.

S: What happened?

T: I remember putting it on the table in the coffee shop. I didn't notice until we left the table.

S: What does it look like?

T: It's brown leather. My credit card and digital camera are inside.

S: Okay. I'll check to see if anyone has found it.

Scene 3 <With the security officer ② >

(S: Security officer   T: Tourist)

S: You should immediately contact the card company to stop your card.

T: I see. Is there anything else I should do?

S: Fill out this form. That way we can contact you.

T: Okay. By the way, do you have GlobalCard's telephone number ?

S: No, we don't. You can ask at information. They may have it.

Unit 11 💿 52

Comprehension Check

Scene 1 <At the station ① >

(S: Station clerk   T: Tourist)

- T: Excuse me. How can I get to Liberty Island?
- S: Take the number 1 line on the subway, which is the yellow…no, red line on the map to South Ferry.
- T: Number 1 Line… I see.
- S: Once you arrive at South Ferry, exit the subway and follow the signs to Castle Clinton. You can get the ferry to Liberty Island there.

Scene 2 <With the bus driver >

(D: Driver   T: Tourist)

- T: Do you go to the Colombia University area?
- D: No, we don't. But you can change buses at 42nd. I can give you a transfer ticket.
- T: How much is the fare?
- D: The fare is two fifty when using a Pay-Per-Ride Metro Card, but if you want to pay in cash each ride, it costs you two seventy-five.
- T: I see. Can I get change?
- D: No. You must pay exact change. No dollar bills.

Scene 3 <At the station ② >

(S: Station clerk   T: Tourist)

- T: I'd like to buy a ticket to Boston.
- S: When would you like to go?
- T: Tomorrow morning.
- S: One way or round trip?
- T: I want to come back on the same day. If I buy a round trip, is it any cheaper?
- S: No, I'm sorry. Prices vary depending on when you reserve and which train you take.

Unit 12 🎧 57

Comprehension Check

Scene 1 <At the bicycle rental shop ① >

(C: Clerk   T: Tourist)

T: Hi, we are interested in renting some bikes.

C: Hi, hello, welcome! We have a variety of options. How long are you looking to rent them for?

T: Well, probably for a few hours. What is the easiest and the cheapest?

C: This bike here is very easy to ride and the rental price is only eight dollars per hour and twenty-five dollars for a half day. A helmet, locks, a basket and a map are included.

T: What about insurance?

C: We have plans starting from five dollars.

Scene 2 <At the bicycle rental shop ② >

(C: Clerk   T: Tourist)

T: Are there any rules when riding?

C: Yes, there are state laws. Bikes are defined as vehicles here.

T: Do you ride on the street?

C: Yes. Not on the sidewalks. There are marked bike lanes or paths. Yield to pedestrians and obey traffic lights.

T: Okay. I understand.

C: I recommend riding in Central Park. It's very nice.

Scene 3 <At the bicycle rental shop ③ >

(C: Clerk   T: Tourist)

T: Excuse me. I got a flat tire! Look at this!

C: Oh, what happened?

T: When I was riding on the path in the park, I noticed that the tire was flat.

C: Oh, no! We pre-inspect every bike carefully before each rental.

T: But it blew out. It wasn't my fault, you see. I'm not happy with this!

C: I understand, but flat tires do happen.

T: Can I get a refund?

C: Unfortunately we can't issue refunds.

Unit 13 🔘 62

Comprehension Check

Scene 1 <On the road ① >

(P: Passer-by   T: Tourist)

T: Sorry to bother you, but can you tell me how to get to Penn Station, please?

P: Sure, from here, it's about a ten-minute walk. Just off Seventh Avenue.

T: Seventh Avenue?

P: Yep. Go straight down this street and it's on the second…no, on the third corner.

T: Thank you.

P: You're welcome. Enjoy your stay.

Scene 2 <On the road ② >

(P1: Passer-by1   P2: Passer-by2   T: Tourist)

T: Well, obviously this isn't the right direction… Excuse me, can you tell me where the nearest post office is?

P1: Sorry, I'm not familiar with this area.

(After a while)

T: Excuse me. How can I get to the post office?

P2: Uhh… Go back to West 14th Street and turn left on Fifth, then keep going until you reach Union Square.

T: That sounds a little complicated.

P2: Well, it's not nearby but it's still within a walking distance. I'd walk. When you get there, you'll see the post office on your right.

Scene 3 <On the road ③ >

(P: Passer-by   T: Tourist)

T: Excuse me, I think I'm lost. Could you show me where I am on the map?

P: Sure. You're here. Where would you like to go specifically?

T: I'd like to go to POWERBOOKS, the famous book store.

P: Oh, sure. Then you go straight up to the traffic light and then turn left.

T: Got it.

P: You'll see it on your left, next to the big supermarket.

T: Great. Thanks for your help!

Unit 14 🎧 67

Comprehension Check

Scene 1 <At the pharmacy>

(P: Pharmacist T: Tourist)

T: I think I've got a cold. I have a sore throat, and my eyes are irritated.

P: I see. Do you have a runny nose?

T: Yes, I do.

P: It sounds like a cold. Are you allergic to any drugs?

T: Well, I don't think so.

P: Then, I'd recommend you take these tablets and cough drops.

T: Okay, how often should I take them?

P: Take two tablets every four hours with water. And you can have one drop every two hours as needed.

Scene 2 <At the hotel>

(H: Hotel clerk T: Tourist)

T: I think I ate something bad at lunch. I've had a stomachache and have been feeling sick all afternoon.

H: Have you taken anything for it?

T: No, nothing.

H: You should see a doctor. Shall I call one for you?

T: Yes, please.

H: While you are waiting, I can make some chamomile tea for you. It should soothe your stomach.

T: Thank you. How long will it take the doctor to get here?

H: I'm not sure but I'll ask.

Scene 3 <At the doctor's office>

(D: Doctor T: Tourist)

T: I think I've twisted my ankle.

D: May I take a look? Oh, it's swollen. It must be painful.

T: Yes, it is.

D: When did you twist it?

T: Hmm, a couple of hours ago.

D: I'll get you a cold bandage and write you a prescription for a pain killer.

T: Could I have a medical certificate for my travel insurance?

Unit 15 🎧 72

Comprehension Check

Scene 1 <At the hotel>

(F: Front clerk T: Tourist)

    F: Did you enjoy your stay with us?

    T: I sure did.

    F: Great. Could I ask you to fill out our questionnaire?

    T: I'd like to, but I overslept and don't have enough time.

    F: It's also available on our website.

    T: All right then, I will fill it out online. Can you call me a taxi?
        I don't have enough time to take a bus.

Scene 2 <In the taxi>

(D: Driver T: Tourist)

    D: That's fifty-five dollars plus a fifteen dollar surcharge for a trip to Newark Airport.

    T: I'm sorry? What is the surcharge?

    D: There's an additional charge for Manhattan to Newark Airport. It's written on the form
        here. To LaGuardia and JFK, the flat rate applies.

    T: Okay, I understand. Here you are. Make it eighty. Just give me back twenty bucks.

    D: Thank you. Get off on the curb side, please. Have a nice flight.

Scene 3 <At the airport>

(C: Check-in clerk T: Tourist)

    C: Your flight will be delayed for about three hours.

    T: No kidding! Do you mean that I can't catch the flight to Japan?

    C: Right. So we have arranged a flight to Toronto for you at no charge.

    T: Through Toronto in Canada?

    C: That's right. The flight is leaving here at 10:45 and arriving at Toronto at 12:15, then you
        change flights to Narita leaving at 2:10 pm, which arrives at Narita at 3:55 pm the next day.

    T: Can you write it down? I didn't catch everything. I'm confused.

image credit

Cover
AleksandarNakic / istockphoto.com

Unit 1   Tupungato / Shutterstock.com   snapgalleria / Shutterstock.com
Unit 2   Stanislaw Tokarski / Shutterstock.com   Artisticco / Shutterstock.com
Unit 3   Pavel L Photo and Video / Shutterstock.com   ChameleonsEye / Shutterstock.com
Unit 4   racorn / Shutterstock.com   KPG Ivary / Shutterstock.com
Unit 5   Nickolay Vinokurov / Shutterstock.com   CoraMax / Shutterstock.com   Leonard Zhukovsky / Shutterstock.com
Unit 6   Radu Bercan / Shutterstock.com   antart / Shutterstock.com
Unit 7   ChameleonsEye / Shutterstock.com   Oleksiy Mark / Shutterstock.com   aerogondo2 / Shutterstock.com
Unit 8   CandyBox Images / Shutterstock.com   Doremi / Shutterstock.com
Unit 9   Olesia Bilkei / Shutterstock.com   Neda Sadreddin / Shutterstock.com
Unit 10 esbobeldijk / Shutterstock.com
Unit 11 Robert Madeira / Shutterstock.com   Christopher Penler / Shutterstock.com
Unit 12 Bikeworldtravel / Shutterstock.com   Gordon Bell / Shutterstock.com
Unit 13 wdstock / istockphoto.com   tovovan / Shutterstock.com   Rob Wilson / Shutterstock.com
Unit 14 Stuart Jenner / Shutterstock.com   Pressmaster / Shutterstock.com
Unit 15 Jaromir Chalabala / Shutterstock.com   Pulsmusic / Shutterstock.com   Lorelyn Medina / Shutterstock.com

著作権法上、無断複写・複製は禁じられています。

Enjoy Your Trip! —English you need abroad—		[B-783]
旅英語の心得		
1 刷	2015年 2月 6日	
10 刷	2024年 3月 29日	
著 者	竹内 真澄	Masumi Takeuchi
	中井 延美	Nobumi Nakai
	菅原 千津	Chizu Sugawara
英文校正		Joseph Tabolt
発行者	南雲 一範　Kazunori Nagumo	
発行所	株式会社　南雲堂	
	〒162-0801　東京都新宿区山吹町361	
	NAN'UN-DO Co., Ltd.	
	361 Yamabuki-cho, Shinjuku-ku, Tokyo 162-0801, Japan	
	振替口座：00160-0-46863	
	TEL：03-3268-2311（営業部：学校関係）	
	03-3268-2384（営業部：書店関係）	
	03-3268-2387（編集部）	
	FAX：03-3269-2486	
編集者	加藤 敦	
製 版	橋本 佳子	
装 丁	Nスタジオ	
検 印	省 略	
コード	ISBN 978-4-523-17783-8　C0082	

Printed in Japan

E-mail　nanundo@post.email.ne.jp
URL　https://www.nanun-do.co.jp/